A New Owner's
Guide to
CHOW CHOWS

JG-131

Overleaf: A Chow adult and puppy owned by Frank and Sandra Holloway.

Opposite page: Magnificent examples of Smooth Chows owned by Dr. Samuel Draper and George and Kat Beliew.

The Publisher wishes to acknowledge the following owners of the dogs in this book: Elaine and Linda Albert, George and Kat Beliew, Michael Bakert, Paulette Braun, Phillip Capozzolo, Teresa Clark, Theresa Corrall, Ernie Coy, Dr. Samuel Draper, Donald Drewwary, Frank and Sandra Holloway, Imagine Chow Kennels, Michael Larissa, Andreeva Liubuv, Karen Lundin, Joel Marston, John Miska, Charlene Niles, Deborah Pederson, Pat Rose.

Photographers: Rick Beauchamp, Booth Photography, Paulette Braun, Tara Darling, Isabelle Francais, Robert Pearcy, Perry Phillips, Vince Serbin, Alex Smith, Judith E. Strom, Dennis Valadez.

The author acknowledges the contribution of Judy Iby for the following chapters: Sport of Purebred Dogs, Identification and Finding the Lost Dog, Traveling with Your Dog, Health Care, Behavior and Canine Communication.

Distributed in the UNITED STATES to the Pet Trade by T.F.H. Publications, Inc., One T.F.H. Plaza, Neptune City, NJ 07753; distributed in the UNITED STATES to the Bookstore and Library Trade by National Book Network, Inc. 4720 Boston Way, Lanham MD 20706; in CANADA to the Pet Trade by H & L Pet Supplies Inc., 27 Kingston Crescent, Kitchener, Ontario N2B 2T6; Rolf C. Hagen Inc., 3225 Sartelon St. Laurent-Montreal Quebec H4R 1E8; in CANADA to the Book Trade by Vanwell Publishing Ltd., 1 Northrup Crescent, St. Catharines, Ontario L2M 6P5 ; in ENGLAND by T.F.H. Publications, PO Box 15, Waterlooville PO7 6BQ; in AUSTRALIA AND THE SOUTH PACIFIC by T.F.H. (Australia), Pty. Ltd., Box 149, Brookvale 2100 N.S.W., Australia; in NEW ZEALAND by Brooklands Aquarium Ltd. 5 McGiven Drive, New Plymouth, RD1 New Zealand; in Japan by T.F.H. Publications, Japan—Jiro Tsuda, 10-12-3 Ohjidai, Sakura, Chiba 285, Japan; in SOUTH AFRICA by Lopis (Pty) Ltd., P.O. Box 39127, Booysens, 2016, Johannesburg, South Africa. Published by T.F.H. Publications, Inc.
MANUFACTURED IN THE
UNITED STATES OF AMERICA
BY T.F.H. PUBLICATIONS, INC.

A NEW OWNER'S GUIDE TO CHOW CHOWS

RICHARD BEAUCHAMP

Contents

1997 Edition

These puppies demonstrate the resemblance between Chows and bear cubs.

A well-cared for Chow will be a healthy and loving companion for many years.

108 - Behavior and Canine Communication

Canine Behavior - Socializing and Training - Understanding the Dog's Language - Body Language - Fear - Aggression - Problems

The Chow is a powerfully built, sturdy dog whose keen intelligence is shown in his expression.

The versatile Chow excels at everything from conformation to therapy work.

142 - Dental Care for Your Dog's Life

148 - Identification and Finding the Lost Dog

Finding the Lost Dog

152 - Traveling With Your Dog

Trips - Air Travel - Boarding Kennels

Although they possess independent natures, Chows thrive on the attention they receive from their owners.

126 - Health Care

The First Check-Up - The Physical Exam - Immunizations - Annual Visit - Intestinal Parasites - Other Intestinal Parasites - External Parasites - To Breed or Not to Breed

HISTORY of the Chow Chow

When the world was being created, what dog was allowed to lick up all the little pieces of blue sky which fell on the earth when the stars were being set in their place? The Chow, said Li Fu, and that is how he got his blue tongue. *From an ancient Chinese fairy tale.* This excerpt from an ancient Chinese fairy story typifies the many romantic tales that surround the history of the uniquely beautiful and temperamentally distinctive Chow Chow. The misty origin of this breed, most often simply referred to as the Chow, has given rise to many tales of legendary qualities and bizarre lineage. Not the least of these legends is the one that claims the bear rather than the wolf as the Chow's ancient ancestor.

While the Chow's relationship to the bear is looked upon as scientifically preposterous by some, others substantiate the claim by citing many of the Chow's characteristics that it shares with no other animal but the bear. When one looks at the bear's independent nature, the stilted manner in which it moves and the remarkable resemblance of the bear cubs to the Chow itself, one can only wonder if Mother Nature might have lent some ironic twist to the evolution of the Chow.

While China embraces the Chow as one of its own, Chinese historical documents consistently refer to the breed in ancient manuscripts and books as "the foreign Chow," substantiating the generally accepted theory that the Chow was not an indigenous breed but one of Arctic origin coming to China

The Chow's majestic stance, regal bearing and independent nature make him one of the most distinctive breeds in America today.

The Chow's existence as a Chinese warrior dog can be traced back to as early as 225 BC. This is Ch. Juli's Red Headed Stranger and Int. Ch. Jujo Satin Nimbus.

along with the barbarian tribes that frequently invaded China in the 11th century BC.

Legend tells of the barbarian invaders' huge dogs with black tongues that were so fierce in nature and strong of body that they could easily bring down the enemy with no assistance. These warrior dogs were sometimes described as closely resembling lions in color as well as in their heads, claws and manes that clothed their necks.

Though the Chow's existence in China can be traced through its image appearing on bronzes and in paintings through the centuries, much of the breed's documented history was destroyed by the Emperor Chin Shih, who wantonly destroyed most of China's literature in 225 BC. The meager records that survived, however, do add some interesting details to the earlier descriptions of the warrior dogs.

These writings describe the dogs as being completely different from other breeds of dog, with large broad heads, short muzzles and small eyes. The lips are described as not overlapping but just touching, giving them a unique aloof expression. While devoted to their owners or keepers, these warrior dogs were extremely hostile toward strangers and predators. In addition to their role as warrior dogs, Chows are also said to have been used for hunting, guarding livestock and even as herding dogs for the huge cattle herds maintained by the barbarian tribes.

Certainly there can be no doubt of the Chow's antiquity, the breed's place of naturalization or its distinctive physical appearance. While there are constant references to the breed throughout China's history, it was not until much later that the breed would actually be referred to as the Chow Chow.

As time progressed, the Chinese were able to lower, if not entirely quench, the flames of the Chow's barbaric temperament. The breed was assigned more domestic duties as draft dog, hunter, herder, guardian of the home and, alas, as food for the family as well.

These adorable puppies demonstrate the remarkable resemblance between Chows and bear cubs. That cuddly quality makes them hard to resist!

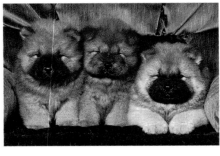

The Chinese slang word for something edible is "chow," and the breed of the same name was noted for the delicacy of its meat, which regularly replaced lamb. Dog meat was sold and eaten throughout China and Korea until it was prohibited by law in China in 1915. In fact, Chinese legend gives us purely utilitarian reasons for two of the Chow's most distinguishing characteristics—it is said the straighter the hind leg, the more abundant the meat; and the bluer the tongue, the sweeter the meat.

THE CHOW IN GREAT BRITAIN

There can be no doubt that as the first clipper ships entered Chinese harbors, British sailors were fascinated by the multitude of curiosities this strange country afforded. Certainly, not the least of these oddities was a dog more bear-

One of the great champion Chow Chows, Ch. Ah Sid The Dilettante, won a total of 26 all-breed Best in Shows and 91 Non-Sporting Group Firsts between 1957 and 1964.

like or lion-like than anything ever seen before by British seamen. It is little wonder that the sailors took these canine curiosities back to England with them on return voyages. In 1780, the first Chows arrived in Great Britain.

Little is known of the fate of those first exotic immigrants to England. It was not until 60 years later that an 1840 newspaper account tells of several Chows that were kept in the London Zoological Park. They were referred to as the "wild dogs of China."

In 1880, however, records document the exhibition of Chinese Puzzle, a black Chow female imported directly from China. Chinese Puzzle was exhibited at a dog show that took place at the Crystal Palace in London. Evidently, the look of

Chinese Puzzle caught the eye and captured the fancy of some of London's more fashionable ladies, including the Marchioness of Huntley.

When the Marchioness was offered a Chow that her relative the Earl of Lonsdale had brought back from China, she not only accepted the gift but immediately requested that the Earl bring back more of the dogs on his next trip.

Immediately upon the arrival of the new dogs, Lady Huntley set about breeding Chows, heading up the kennel with an imported male she named Periodot.

Int. Ch. Bearkat Buckwheat, owned by Paulette Braun, looks right at home in this Oriental setting.

Periodot II, a Periodot daughter who was bred by the Marchioness, was subsequently sold to Lady Granville Gordon who established a highly respected breeding kennel on the blood of this female. Lady Gordon was followed in her interest in the Chow Chow by her daughter, Lady Faudel Phillips, who was to become the most important and influential breeder in England. The Ladies Gordon and Phillips were to produce the first English- bred champion Chow who was named simply Blue Blood.

The English Chow Chow Club was established in 1895 at which time the first standard for the breed was written. The first show for the breed was held at Westminster in London that same year.

When Lady Gordon died, Lady Phillips fell heir to all of the Chows. With these dogs and some of her own, Lady Phillips established the legendary Amwell Chow Chow Kennel in 1919. The kennel was to remain in operation until Lady Phillips's death in 1943.

With the breed in the hands of England's wealthy and titled men and women, the Chow Chow flourished. The breed's fanciers could well afford huge kennels

The Chow Chow's image has been represented in many different forms of art, including this copper statue done by Hiroshi Takagi of Japan.

and the talented stockmen it took to manage them. The breed grew both in number and in quality.

The first Chow to become an English champion was an import, Ch. Chow VIII, which was described as a dog of good type though somewhat lacking in coat. Unfortunately, Chow VIII had a temperament that left much to be desired. Though his nasty temperament resulted in frequent changes of ownership, it barely affected Chow VIII's show career, which was somewhat spectacular for the day. Temperament notwithstanding, it is believed that England's standard of the breed was written with Chow VIII as its model.

As years progressed, word of these mighty and exotic dogs spread to Europe and to America. In Europe, it became a mark of distinction among the wealthy to own one of the edible "wild dogs of China." While high prices were paid for Chow Chows in Europe, the breed was not really accepted there by serious dog fanciers until many years later.

In England, the Chow Chow was forced to survive the devastating effects of two world wars. With the determination so typical of the English, fanciers not only helped the breed inch forward through the worst of times but actually brought the breed to a resplendent level of quality shortly after World War II. There can be no doubt that the breed owes its celebrated status throughout the world to England and the great dog men and women there who embraced the edible "wild dog of China" and shaped it into the loved and respected breed it is today.

THE BREED IN AMERICA

As the Chow increased in number and quality in Great Britain, the breed was attracting a mighty following in America as well. The first Chow exhibited in the United States appeared at the Westminster Kennel Club show in 1890.

According to famed breeder and breed historian Dr. Samuel Draper, 1905 is the most important date to be noted in the breed's American history. In that year, Mrs. Charles E. Proctor founded her Blue Dragon Kennels and imported Chinese Chum, a dog who was destined to become America's first champion Chow. Veterans of the breed consider Ch. Chinese Chum to be the cornerstone of the breed in the United States. Dr. and Mrs. Henry Jarrett had also established a kennel in Philadelphia and campaigned their dogs throughout the East.

In 1906, the Jarretts were instrumental in founding the Chow Chow Club, Inc., the parent club of the breed.

As in England, World War I had its deleterious effect upon dog shows and dog breeding in the US. While enthusiasts maintained their devotion to the breed, activity came to a near standstill. There was, however, a marked acceleration of interest in the breed in the 1920s. This popularity was undoubtedly due in a great part to the fact that a Chow was living in the White House with President Calvin Coolidge. Unfortunately, this upsurge in popularity was to prove disastrous to the character and the image of the inscrutable Chow Chow.

Today's Chow Chows are noted for their nobility of character and handsome appearance. "Billy" and "Yoda" are shining examples.

Unscrupulous breeders attempted to capitalize on the Chow craze by launching full scale breeding programs with no concern given to the suitability of the bloodlines they were using. Nor was there any attempt made

to do the necessary socialization with the resulting offspring. The Chow market was flooded with ill-bred and ill-tempered stock. Soon the breed was overcome by nasty spirited dogs earning the breed a reputation as not only untrustworthy but in some cases downright dangerous.

Those who truly loved the breed were left to live down this damaged reputation and re-educate the general public as to how great a companion a well-bred Chow could be. Certainly assisting in this endeavor were Ch. Yang Fu Tang, the great winner of the 1930s who won 22 all-breed Bests in Show, and Lle Wol Lah Son, who won the Non-Sporting Group at the Westminster Kennel Club dog show in 1940. No other Chow would win a Group at Westminster until 1969 when the red male Ch. Gotschall's Van Van did so under the esteemed all-breed judge Alva Rosenberg.

It is to the credit of Chow Chow breeders and fanciers of the

No Chow had won a Group at Westminster until Ch. Gotschall's Van Van in 1969, owned by Donald L. Drewwary and bred by Valetta Gotschall.

Joel Marston, one of the breeders credited with improving the image and temperament of the Chow Chow, poses with Ch. Starcrest Mr. Christopher in 1973.

1950s and 1960s throughout America that great emphasis was placed upon the temperament and image of the breed. Great strides were made in these areas by one and all, but certainly particular credit must be given to both Joel Marston (Starcrest Chow Chows) and Dr. Samuel Draper (Liontamer Chow Chows) who bred dogs of superior type and great temperament on opposite coasts of the US.

The dogs bred and owned by these two gentlemen were of unquestionable character, and although at times the two were competitors in the ring, they were completely united in their efforts to re-establish the Chow as a human companion of merit. Draper and Marston were great ambassadors of the breed and new friends were made for the Chow wherever these two men or their dogs would appear. Certainly the Chow fancy owes a great debt of gratitude to these dedicated men who led the compatible Chow movement in America.

The Chow Chow of today has risen above its ill-gotten reputation of the past and stands proudly among man's most popular and devoted companions. For the person who takes the time to truly understand the character of the Chow Chow, there can be no greater canine friend.

15

CHARACTERISTICS of the Chow Chow

As we already know, all puppies are cute. Not all puppies grow up to be particularly attractive adults, though. What is considered beauty by one person is not necessarily seen as attractive by another. It is almost impossible to determine what a mixed breed puppy will look like as an adult. Nor will it be possible to determine if the mixed breed puppy's temperament is suitable for the person or family who wishes to own it. If the puppy grows up to be too big, too hairy or too active for the owner, what will happen to it?

All puppies are irresistible, and Chows are certainly no exception. However, make sure the Chow will fit into your home and lifestyle before making the commitment to own one.

Size and temperament can vary to a degree even with purebred dogs. Still, selective breeding over many generations has produced dogs that give the would-be owner reasonable assurance of what the purebred puppy will look and act like as an adult. Attractiveness completely aside, this predictability is more important than one might think.

A person who wants a dog to go along on those morning jogs or long distance runs is not going to be particularly happy with a lethargic or short-legged breed. Nor is the fastidious housekeeper, whose picture of the ideal dog is one which lies quietly at the feet of its master by the hour and never sheds, going to be particularly happy with the shaggy dog whose temperament is reminiscent of a hurricane.

Purebred puppies will grow up to look like their adult relatives and by and large they will behave pretty much like the rest of their family. Any dog, mixed breed or not, has

The Chow has is extremely intelligent and eager to please, but at the same time, very stubborn. If a Chow decides he likes you, he'll be your friend for life.

the potential to be a loving companion. However, a purebred dog offers reasonable insurance that it will not only suit the owner's lifestyle but the person's esthetic demands as well.

PERSONALITY OF THE CHOW

The Chow character is as unique as it is contradictory. Housebreaking takes half the time, if that, of any other breed I have ever tried to take through the same procedure. It's a lesson the Chowlet seems to want to learn and, once learned, only a major catastrophe can get the adult to transgress.

On the other hand, the breed has a stubborn streak a mile long. The experienced Chow owner knows how quickly the average Chow understands what you are trying to teach it. The same owner also knows how long it can be before the understanding Chow chooses to comply. This stubbornness extends itself to what the Chow learns. Avoid like the plague the development of bad habits. Once learned, it takes the devil to pay before you will be able to convince your Chow to forget that bad habit.

Most Chows look at strangers on a take it or leave it basis. It is fine if their masters decide to have friends come to call; just as fine if not. Our Chow "Blossom" would have been just as content had we never bothered entertaining at all. When company did arrive, however, she was betwixt and between. On the one hand, she would have been perfectly happy to retire to another room, but her innate curiosity compelled her to be present for whatever might happen. She resolved the matter by positioning herself in the doorway of the room where our guests had gathered but with her rear end facing the guests while she pretended to gaze indifferently into another room.

As indifferent as the Chow can be to the comings and goings of visitors, woe to the would-be intruder! The most lethargic appearing Chow can suddenly become a hurricane of protectiveness.

Chows seem to make blanket judgments. If your Chow sees the little girl next door as a kind and gentle playmate, all little children are apt to be high on its list of favorite things. Conversely, if the uniformed utilities man threatens or kicks your Chow, pity any uniformed man who enters your premises! Therefore, it is wise to make sure your Chow's initial introduction to people is a positive experience. You will be hard pressed to change your Chow's mind once it is made up. This applies to change in ownership as well. A good many of the breeds I have bred and owned are just as happy living in one place as another, just so long as they are well fed and are well treated. My Boxers were ecstatic when they realized we were approaching the boarding kennel where they sometimes stayed while I was to be away on an extended trip. My Cockers had favorite people among my acquaintances who they would have gladly departed with had they only been invited to do so. Not so with the Chow!

One of the most heartbreaking situations I was ever forced to experience had to do with the rehoming of Blossom, the Chow which had grown up as a constant companion. An unexpected professional change made it necessary to give her up but I felt fortunate to have found her a new home with a kind and loving person. The new owner did everything possible to assist a happy transition but it was to no avail. Blossom pined continually even through the birth of a litter of puppies, which she dealt with in a purely perfunctory manner. It was not too long afterward that she died. The veterinarian said her death was due to cancer. That was the medical profession's explanation for her death. Those who had lived with Blossom know she died of a broken heart.

Introduce your Chow puppy to all different types of people, especially children. The more people they meet, the better socialized they become.

Have I made Chow ownership sound like a challenge? If so, you have definitely taken my message. There is no doubt at all that a Chow will be able to test you in every way possible, but I am inclined to believe it is all done to determine whether or not you are worthy of being a Chow

owner. If you do qualify, you will have a companion the likes of which you will never forget.

WHO SHOULD OWN A CHOW?

What kind of person should own a Chow? One word will describe this person—patient. If the Chow owner is patient he will be rewarded with a companion whose devotion knows no end and whose sense of humor knows no bounds.

Chows are excellent companions whose devotion knows no bounds. If you want an independent dog with a great sense of humor, the Chow is the breed for you!

I assure you, the Chow is like no other dog. Lady Dunbar of Mochrum, one of England's pioneer breeders of the Chow, described the breed as follows, "...The Chow has many noble qualities, his heart cannot be taken by storm, but, once given, it is yours forever..." Though written in the early years of the 20th century, this description of the Chow's character remains as apt today as it was then.

I have owned many breeds of dog. None has been so independent, so humorous, so disdainful of strangers or so absolutely devoted as the Chow. If molding a dog's spirit to conform to your picture of the ideal canine companion is an important factor in dog ownership, consider a breed other than the Chow. You can guide a Chow in the direction you want it to go but you can't push it there. Nor can you be heavy handed, as rough and tumble as the breed may be. As sturdy a constitution as the Chow may have and

as high as its tolerance for discomfort might be, a Chow is completely incapable of being struck in anger. This devastates the Chow, and if subjected to treatment of this nature on a continuing basis,

The Chow has a number of unique qualities that makes him a friendly and versatile breed.

even the most amiable youngster can be turned into a neurotic and unpredictable adult.

This is not to say that the Chow owner needs to or should be passive in raising and training a Chow. On the contrary, a Chowlet must start understanding household rules from the first moment it comes into your home. What it will take to accomplish this is the aforementioned patience and a firm but gentle hand. This does not mean that a well-placed slap on the rump with a folded newspaper can never be administered. Somehow even the youngest Chowlet understands the difference between being corrected and being abused.

Someone who needs a dog that does well living outdoors with minimal owner interaction should in all fairness also look to another breed. The Chow must have constant human companionship and social interaction not only with its owner but with all kinds of people and other dogs. The Chow raised without this socialization can easily become introverted and sullen. The young Chow can pass through an adolescent stage where it decides that its owner or family is all that is necessary to its well-being and can become very anti-social unless made to understand this is unacceptable.

It is then up to the caring owner to help guide the Chow through this difficult stage. Patience,

The Chow is a very social animal who needs to interact with people in order to thrive. Rebelrun's Mountain Sun is ready to "play ball" with whoever wants to join the fun.

22

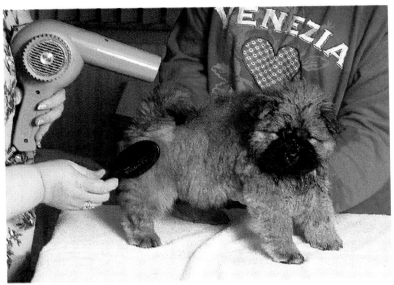

In terms of grooming, the rough Chow is a high maintenance dog. If grooming is a concern, consider a smooth Chow — the responsibilities are much less involved.

persistence and support will help your Chow through this awkward time, but it does take time and commitment to stay out there with the "bashful" youngster.

Needless to say, the Chow owner must be prepared to take care of the breed's coat. The would-be Chow owner is able to predetermine how much time he will spend on coat care in that the breed comes in two coat varieties: smooth and rough. The heavier the coat, the more time and effort will be required. This is particularly so when the Chowlet begins to shed out its puppy coat and the new adult hair begins to grow. Mats and tangles seem to appear from one minute to the next. While the coat becomes more manageable as the Chow matures, the responsible owner should allow an hour or so at least twice a week to keep the mature rough Chow's coat tangle free and healthy. The smooth and rough Chows are exactly the same breed and the choice between the two is purely esthetic or perhaps weighted by the amount of time available to devote to your Chow's grooming.

STANDARD of the Chow Chow

General Appearance—*Characteristics*—An ancient breed of northern Chinese origin, this all-purpose dog of China was originally used for hunting, herding, pulling and protection of the home. While primarily a companion and family dog today, his working origin must always be remembered when assessing true Chow Chow type.

A powerful, sturdy, squarely built, upstanding dog of Arctic type, medium in size with strong muscular development and heavy bone. The body is compact, short coupled, broad and deep, the tail set high and carried closely to the back, the whole supported by four straight, strong, sound legs. Viewed from the side, the hind legs have little apparent angulation and

A medium-sized, powerfully built, sturdy dog, the Chow Chow's working origins are evident in the breed today.

the hock joint and metatarsals are directly beneath the hip joint. It is this structure which produces the characteristic short, stilted gait unique to the breed. The large head with broad, flat skull and short, broad and deep muzzle is proudly carried and accentuated by a ruff. Elegance and substance must be combined into a well balanced whole, never so massive as to outweigh his ability to be active, alert and agile. Clothed in a smooth or an offstanding rough double coat, the Chow is a masterpiece of beauty, dignity and naturalness, unique in his blue-black tongue, scowling expression and stilted gait.

Size, Proportions, Substance—*Size*—The average height of adult specimens is 17 to 20 inches at the withers but in every case consideration of overall proportions and type should take precedence over size.

The Chow's large, flat head and blue-black tongue are two of his most distinctive features.

Proportions—Square in profile and close coupled. Distance from forechest to point of buttocks equals height at the highest points of the withers. *Serious Fault*—Profile other than square. Distance from tip of elbow to ground is half the height at the withers. Floor of chest level with tips of elbows. Width viewed from the front and rear is the same and must be broad. It is these proportions that are essential to true Chow type. In judging puppies, no allowance should be made for their failure to conform to these proportions.

Substance—Medium in size with strong muscular development and heavy bone. Equally objectionable are snipy, fine boned specimens and overdone, ponderous, cloddy specimens. In comparing specimens of different sex, due allowance must be made in favor of the bitches who may not have as much head or substance as do the males. There is an impression of femininity in bitches as compared to an impression of masculinity in dogs.

Head—Proudly carried, large in proportion to the size of the dog but never so exaggerated as to make the dog seem top-heavy or to result in a low carriage.

Bearing a more-than-passing resemblance to a lion, the Chow's scowling expression and deep-set eyes give him a lordly air.

Expression essentially scowling, dignified, lordly, discerning, sober and snobbish, one of independence. The scowl is achieved by a marked brow with a padded button of skin just above the inner, upper corner of each eye; by sufficient play of skin to form frowning brows and a distinct furrow between the eyes beginning at the base of the muzzle and extending up the forehead; by the correct eye shape and placement and by the correct ear shape, carriage and placement. Excessive loose skin is not desirable. Wrinkles on the muzzle do not contribute to expression and are not required.

Eyes dark brown, deep set and placed wide apart and obliquely, of moderate size, almond in shape. The correct placement and shape should create an Oriental appearance. The eye rims black with lids which neither turn in nor droop and the pupils of the eyes clearly visible. *Serious Faults—* Entropion or ectropion, or pupils wholly or partially obscured by loose skin. *Ears* small, moderately thick, triangular in shape with a slight rounding at the tip, carried stiffly erect but with a slight forward tilt. Placed wide apart with the inner corner on top of the skull. An ear which flops as the dog moves is very undesirable. *Disqualifying Fault—*Drop ear or ears. A drop ear is one which breaks at any point from its base to its tip or which is not carried stiffly erect but lies parallel to the top of the skull.

The Chow Chow's nose and mouth should be solid black. A pink tongue would be grounds for disqualification.

*Skull—*The top skull is broad and flat from side to side and front to back. Coat and loose skin cannot substitute for the correct bone structure. Viewed in profile, the toplines of the muzzle and skull are approximately parallel, joined by a moderate stop. The padding of the brows may make the stop appear steeper than it is. The muzzle is short in comparison to the length of the top skull but never less than one-third of the head length. The muzzle is broad and well filled out under the eyes, its width and depth are equal and both dimensions should appear to be the same from its base to its tip. This square appearance is achieved by correct bone structure plus padding of the muzzle and full cushioned lips. The muzzle should never be so padded or cushioned as to make it appear other than square in shape. The upper lips completely cover the lower lips when the mouth is closed but should not be pendulous.

*Nose—*large, broad and black in color with well opened nostrils. *Disqualifying Fault—*Nose spotted or distinctly other color than black, except in blue Chows which may have solid blue or slate noses. *Mouth and Tongue*—Edges of the lips black, tissues of the mouth mostly black, gums preferably black. A solid black mouth is ideal. The top surface and edges of the tongue a solid blue-black, the darker the better. *Disqualifying Fault*—The top surface of edges of the tongue red or pink or with one or more spots of red or pink. *Teeth*—strong and even with a scissors bite.

A purebred Chow should have a strong, well-muscled neck, a broad, deep chest, and perfectly straight forelegs.

Neck, Topline, Body—*Neck* strong, full, well muscled, nicely arched and of sufficient length to carry the head proudly above the topline when standing at attention. *Topline* straight, strong and level from the withers to the root of the tail.

Body short, compact, close coupled, strongly muscled, broad, deep and well let down in the flank. The body, back, coupling and croup must all be short to give the required square build. *Chest* broad, deep and muscular, never narrow or slab-sided. The ribs close together and well sprung, not barrel. The spring of the front ribs is somewhat narrowed at their lower ends to permit the shoulder and upper arm to fit smoothly against the chest wall. The floor of the chest is broad and deep extending down to the tips of the elbows. The point of sternum slightly in front of the shoulder points. *Serious Faults* Labored or abdominal breathing (not to include normal panting), narrow or slab-sided chest. *Loin* well muscled, strong, short, broad and deep. *Croup* short and broad with powerful rump and thigh muscles giving a level croup. *Tail* set high and carried closely to the back at all times, following the line of the spine at the start.

Forequarters—*Shoulders* strong, well muscled, the tips of the shoulder blades moderately close together; the spine of the shoulder forms an angle approximately 55 degrees with the horizontal and forms an angle with the upper arm of approximately 110 degrees, resulting in less reach of the forelegs. Length of upper arm never less than length of shoulder blade. Elbow joints set well back alongside the chest wall, elbows turning neither in nor out. *Forelegs* perfectly straight from elbow to foot with heavy bone which must be in

proportion to the rest of the dog. Viewed from the front, the forelegs are parallel and widely spaced commensurate with the broad chest. *Pasterns*–short and upright. Wrists shall not knuckle over. The dewclaws may be removed. *Feet*–round, compact, catlike, standing well up on the thick toe pads.

Hindquarters–The rear assembly is broad, powerful, and well muscled in the hips and thighs, heavy in bone with rear and front bone approximately equal. Viewed from the rear, the legs are straight, parallel and widely spaced, commensurate with the broad pelvis. *Stifle Joint*–shows little angulation, is well knit and stable, points straight forward and the bones of the joint should be clean and sharp. The *Hock Joint* well let down and appears almost straight. The hock joint must be strong, well knit and firm, never bowing or breaking forward or to either side. The hock joint and metatarsals lie in a straight line below the hip joint. *Serious Faults*–Unsound stifle or hock joints. *Metatarsals*–short and perpendicular to the ground. The dewclaws may be removed. *Feet*–same as front.

An example of a smooth adult, "Buckwheat" and a rough puppy, "Naughty." Owned by Paulette Braun and Karen Lundin.

Coat—There are two types of coat; rough and smooth. Both are double coated. *Rough*—In the rough coat, the outer coat is abundant, dense, straight and offstanding, rather coarse in texture; the undercoat soft, thick and wooly. Puppy coat soft, thick and wooly overall. The coat forms a profuse ruff around the head and neck, framing the head. The coat and ruff is generally longer in dogs than in bitches. Tail well feathered. The coat length varies markedly on different Chows and thickness, texture and condition should be given greater emphasis than length. Obvious trimming or shaping is undesirable. Trimming of the whiskers, feet and metatarsals optional. *Smooth*—The smooth coated Chow is judged by the same standard as the rough coated Chow except that references to the quantity and distribution of the outer coat are not applicable to the smooth coated Chow, which has a hard, dense, smooth outer coat with a definite undercoat. There should be no obvious ruff or feathering on the legs or tail.

The Chow's gait is straight and agile, with the rear gait short and stilted. Although not very quick, the Chow possesses high endurance because of the efficient use of his power.

Color—Clear colored, solid or solid with lighter shadings in the ruff, tail and featherings. There are five colors in the Chow: red (light golden to deep mahogany), black, blue, cinnamon (light fawn to deep cinnamon) and cream. Acceptable colors to be judged on an equal basis.

Gait—Proper movement is the crucial test of proper conformation and soundness. It must be sound, straight moving, agile, brief, quick and powerful, never lumbering. The rear gait short and stilted because of the straighter rear assembly. It is from the side that the unique stilted action is most easily assessed. The rear leg moves up and forward from the hip in a straight, stilted pendulum-like line with a slight bounce in the rump, the legs extend neither far forward nor far backward. The hind foot has a strong thrust which transfers power to the body in an almost straight line due to the minimal rear leg angulation. To transmit this power efficiently to the front assembly, the coupling must be short and there should be

31

no roll through the midsection. Viewed from the rear, the line of bone from hip joint to pad remains straight as the dog moves. As the speed increases the hind legs incline slightly inward. The stifle joints must point in the line of travel, not outward resulting in a bowlegged appearance nor hitching in under the dog. Viewed from the front, the line of bone from shoulder joint to pad remains straight as the dog moves. As the speed increases, the forelegs do not move in exact parallel planes, rather, incline slightly inward. The front legs must not swing out in semicircles nor mince or show any evidence of hackney action. The front and rear assemblies must be in dynamic equilibrium. Somewhat lacking in speed, the Chow has excellent endurance because the sound, straight rear leg provides direct, usable power efficiently.

Temperament–Keen intelligence, an independent spirit and innate dignity give the Chow an aura of aloofness. It is a Chow's nature to be reserved and discerning with strangers. Displays of aggressions or timidity are unacceptable. Because of its deep set eyes the Chow has limited peripheral vision and is best approached within the scope of that vision.

Summary–Faults shall be penalized in proportion to their deviation from the standard. In judging the Chow, the overall picture is of primary consideration. Exaggeration of any characteristic at the expense of balance or soundness shall be severely penalized.

Type should include general appearance, temperament, the harmony of all parts, and soundness, especially as seen when the dog is in motion. There should be proper emphasis on movement, which is the final test of the Chow's conformation, balance and soundness.

Disqualifications

Drop ear or ears. A drop ear is one which breaks at any point from its base to its tip or which

The Chow's intelligence can be seen in his expression. It is marked by a sufficient play of skin to form a frown at the brows.

32

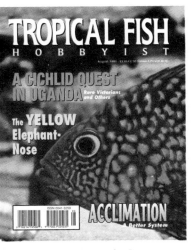

Since 1952, Tropical Fish Hobbyist has been the source of accurate, up-to-the-minute, and fascinating information on every facet of the aquarium hobby. Join the more than 60,000 devoted readers worldwide who wouldn't miss a single issue.

Subscribe right now so you don't miss a single copy!

BRAND NEW: The Best Herp Magazine in the Business!

REPTILE
H O B B Y I S T

CARPET
PYTHONS

Ribbon Snakes
Frilled Dragons
Emerald Swifts

ISSN 0041-3259

***Reptile Hobbyist* is the source for accurate, up-to-the-minute, practical information on *every* facet of the herpetological hobby. Join many thousands of devoted readers worldwide who wouldn't miss a single valuable issue.**

Subscribe right now so you don't miss a single copy!

Some breeds change drastically in appearance from puppyhood to adulthood, but not the Chow. As you can see, Chow puppies resemble the adults very closely. is not carried stiffly erect but lies parallel to the top of the skull. Nose spotted or distinctly other color than black, except in blue Chows which may have solid blue or slate noses. The top surface or edges of the tongue red or pink or with one or more spots of red or pink.

AN OVERVIEW OF THE CHOW CHOW STANDARD

The standard of the Chow Chow is written in a simple straightforward manner that can be read and understood by even the beginning fancier. It takes many years, however, to fully grasp all of its implications. This can only be accomplished though observation of many Chows and reading as much about the breed as possible. What follows is meant to assist the beginning fancier to develop a sense of the important characteristics of the breed.

There are some breeds that change drastically from puppyhood to adulthood. It would be extremely difficult for the novice to determine the actual breed of some dogs in puppyhood, as purebred as the puppies might be. This is not so with the Chowlet. At eight weeks of age, a Chow puppy will look in miniature very much what it will look like as an adult.

33

Above all, the Chow is a squarely built, stalwart looking dog. Its body, measured from breastbone to buttocks, squares with its height at the top of the shoulder (withers). Looking at the Chow in profile, the distance from the withers to the bottom of the chest is the same as from the bottom of the chest to the ground. A short-legged Chow is totally contrary to the very essence of a breed whose origin lies in the snowbound Arctic. Thinking of a dog that must survive in snow country gives you many clues as to just how this sturdy dog should look.

An Arctic dog must have a weather-protective coat, which both the rough and smooth Chow do have. The rough Chow simply has longer hair, but both varieties have thick, straight hair that is coarse and weather resistant.

Large hanging ears would serve no purpose for the Arctic dog. Outsize ears would prove a hindrance, easily freezing in sub-zero weather. Thus the Chow standard asks for stiffly carried small ears. So important are the Chow's small ears that a large ear that is not held erect constitutes a "disqualifying" fault that would bar the dog from being shown.

One of the Chow's distinctive features is its heavy boned gun-barrel-straight legs, which are set at the four corners of its body. When you pick up most other breeds they "give," folding into your arms. Not so with the Chow. There is very little give to their bodies at all—it is rather like picking up a box!

The Chow's large, proudly carried head is another of the breed's obvious and distinctive features. Even though the Chow is a good-sized breed in itself, the head appears large in proportion to the body. The muzzle is short and broad. The skull is large, broad and flat. The nose must be black except in

The Chow is essentially an Arctic dog that is built for cold temperatures. Ch. Mishka Sweetpea of Rebelrun is enjoying her first snowfall.

the case of the blue Chow in which an allowance is made for a blue or slate-colored nose. Otherwise, a pink, gray-colored or pink-spotted nose constitutes another of the Chow's disqualifications. The lips and inside of the Chow's mouth should be black. The top of the tongue must be black. A red or pink tongue or one that is even spotted with those colors would also represent a disqualifying fault.

Be careful to support your Chow's hindquarters when picking him up. His stick-straight legs will not "give" easily.

In total, the Chow's head is massive and its expression is scowling and aloof. This gives the breed the inscrutable and dignified leonine look so typical of the Chow Chow.

The leonine look is typical of the Chow Chow. This is Ch. Rebelrun Teddy Mactyke.

SELECTING Your New Chow Chow

If you are still in the "deciding" stage of whether or not you should bring a Chow puppy into your life, my advice is do not, I repeat do not, visit a kennel or home in which there are Chow Chow puppies. You will not be able to leave without one! Chow puppies are absolutely irresistible. To this day, I immediately remove myself when I see someone coming toward me carrying a Chow puppy. At one time or another I have either judged, bred or owned dogs of practically every breed known to man. None, however, is as appealing as the little Chow puppy. It is for this very reason that the person anticipating owning a Chow must give serious thought to the decision. All puppies are picture-postcard cuddly and cute, and Chow puppies are particularly so. One will often hear of Chow puppies referred to as "Chowlets." To tell the truth, I do not know what the word

The Chow puppies' teddy bear appeal make them absolutely irresistible— but it is very important to understand the responsibilities involved in raising a Chow before buying one.

Who could not possibly help but fall in love with a sleeping "Chowlet?" actually means or what the person had in mind when he coined the description, but it fits—perfectly.

There is nothing more seductive than a litter of puppies nestled together sound asleep, one on top of the other. But in addition to being cute, puppies are living, breathing and very mischievous little creatures and they are entirely dependent upon their human owners for everything once they leave their mother and littermates.

Buying a dog, especially a puppy, before someone is absolutely sure that he wants to make that commitment can be a serious mistake. The prospective dog owner must clearly understand the amount of time and work involved in dog ownership. Failure to understand the extent of commitment that dog ownership involved is one of the primary reasons why there are so many unwanted canines that end their lives in animal shelters.

Before anyone contemplates the purchase of a dog there are some very important conditions that must be considered. One of the first important questions that must be answered is whether or not the person who will ultimately be responsible for the dog's care and well-being actually wants a dog.

All too often it is the mother of the household who must shoulder the responsibility of the family dog's day-to-day care. While the children in the family, and perhaps even the father, may be wildly enthusiastic about having a dog, it must be remembered that they are away most of the day at school or at work. It is often "mom" who will be taking on the additional responsibility of primary care-giver for the family dog.

It is not a good idea to give a puppy as a gift, but if you do, make sure the recipient is ready and willing to take on the commitment of owning a Chow.

Pets are a wonderful method of teaching children responsibility, but it should be remembered that the enthusiasm that inspires children to promise anything in order to have a new puppy may quickly wane. Who will take care of the puppy once the novelty wears off? Does that person want a dog?

Desire to own a dog aside, does the lifestyle of the family actually provide for responsible dog ownership? If the entire family is away from home from early morning to late at night, who will provide for all of the puppy's needs? Feeding, exercise, outdoor access and the like can not be provided if no one is home.

A pet may be a good way to teach a child responsibility, but not at the expense of the dog. Make sure that all members of the family are willing to take responsibility for your Chow, because he will need proper care and attention.

Another important factor to consider is whether or not the breed of dog is suitable for the person or the family with which it will be living. Some breeds can handle the rough and tumble play of young children. Some can not. On the other hand, some dogs are so large and clumsy, especially as puppies,

No matter what the color, all Chow puppies are equally adorable!

that they could easily and unintentionally injure an infant. Then, too, there is the matter of the hair. A luxuriously coated dog is certainly beautiful to behold, but all of that hair takes a great deal of care. In the case of a rough Chow, an occasional quick going-over with a brush will not suffice. Brushing an adult Chow requires time and a great deal of elbow grease. Both long and short-hairdo dogs shed their coats in the home. Naturally, the longer the hair, the more noticeable it will be. In the case of the Chow, both coats can carry seemingly half the woods or beach along with them when they return after a day's outing. As great as claims are for any breed's intelligence and trainability, remember that the new dog must be taught every household rule that it is to observe. Some dogs catch on more quickly than others and puppies are just as inclined to forget or disregard lessons as young human children.

Having satisfactorily answered all the questions relating to responsible Chow ownership, the prospective owner will undoubtedly want to rush out and purchase a puppy immediately. Do not act in haste. The purchase of any dog is an important step since the well-cared-for dog will live with you for many years. In the case of a Chow this could be 12, 14 or even 15 years. You will undoubtedly want the dog that lives with you for that length of time to be one that you will enjoy.

CHOW CHOW BREEDERS

It is especially important in this breed that your Chow is purchased from a breeder who has earned a reputation over the years for consistently producing dogs that are mentally and physically sound. The Chow is enduring a new wave of worldwide popularity. With this upsurge in interest comes those who are ready and willing to exploit the breed for financial gain with no thought given to the health or welfare of the dogs, or to the homes in which they will be living.

Reputable breeders will be selective in choosing which adult Chows to breed, in order to produce the best puppies possible.

The only way a breeder will earn a reputation for quality is through a well thought out breeding program in which rigid selectivity is imposed. Selective breeding is aimed at maintaining the virtues of a breed and eliminating genetic weaknesses. This process is time consuming and costly. Therefore, responsible Chow breeders protect their investments by providing the utmost in prenatal care for their brood matrons and maximum care and nutrition for the resulting offspring. Once the puppies arrive, the knowledgeable breeder initiates a well thought out socialization process.

The governing kennel clubs in the different countries of the world maintain lists of local breed clubs and breeders that can lead a prospective dog buyer to responsible breeders of quality stock. Should you not be sure of where to contact a respected breeder in your area, we strongly recommend contacting your kennel club for recommendations.

There is every possibility that a reputable breeder resides in your area who will not only be able to provide the right Chow for you, but who will often have the parents of the puppy on the premises as well. This gives you an opportunity to see firsthand what kind of dogs are in the background of the puppy you are considering. Good breeders are not only willing to have you see their dogs but to inspect the facilities in which the dogs are raised as well. These breeders will also be able to discuss problems that exist in the breed with you and how they deal with these problems.

Do not be surprised if a concerned breeder asks many questions about you and the environment in which your Chow will be raised. A responsible breeder will want to know if you have a fenced yard, if there are young children in the family and if someone will be home with the young puppy during the course of an average day. Good breeders are just as concerned with the quality of the homes to which their dogs are going as you, the buyer, are in obtaining a sound and healthy dog.

All this is not to imply that a good Chow puppy can only come from a large kennel. On the contrary, today many of the best breeders raise dogs in their homes as a hobby. Their names may just as easily be included in the recommended lists obtained from kennel clubs as names of people who maintain many dogs. These hobby breeders are equally dedicated to producing quality Chows and in many cases have even more opportunity to devote to the all-important socialization process. Again, it is important that both the buyer and the seller ask questions. I would be highly suspect of a person who is willing to sell you a Chow puppy "no questions asked."

CHOICE OF COAT TYPES

An important consideration that must be addressed is whether at least one of your Chow's owners is willing to assume the responsibility of coat care. To divide this

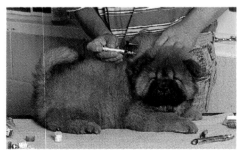

Puppies are especially vulnerable to infectious diseases, so your Chowlet needs to be fully inoculated before being taken out of its home environment.

responsibility among unwilling members of the family is sheer folly. The task will not be done or if it is done at all, not done properly.

As much as we admire the properly groomed rough Chow's crowning glory, one must be realistic and understand that the coat looks that way only because it is given proper care. Fortunately, Chow lovers who do not want the additional responsibility of the rough coat have the option of selecting a smooth Chow puppy or adult. In this case, you have all of the Chow benefits without the work of maintaining that beautiful coat.

Examine the puppy you are considering away from its littermates and choose a puppy with a happy demeanor and healthy appearance. You'll be glad you did!

RECOGNIZING A HEALTHY PUPPY

Most breeders do not release their puppies until the puppies have been given their "puppy shots." Normally, this is at about eight weeks of age. By this time the litter is entirely weaned. Nursing puppies receive a form of maternal immunization from their mother. Once weaned, however, a puppy is highly susceptible to many infectious diseases that can be transmitted via the hands and clothing of people. Therefore, it behooves you to make sure your puppy is fully inoculated before it leaves its home environment.

Above all, the Chowlet you buy should be a happy and bouncy extrovert. The worst thing you could possibly do is buy a "shy violet" puppy or one that appears sick and listless because you feel sorry for it. Doing this will undoubtedly lead to heartache and difficulty, to say nothing of the veterinary costs that you may incur in getting the puppy well.

If at all possible, take the puppy you are interested in away from its littermates into another room or another part of the kennel. The smells will remain the same for the puppy so it should still feel secure and maintain its outgoing personality, but it will give you an opportunity to inspect the puppy more closely. A healthy little Chowlet will be strong and sturdy to the touch, neither bony nor obese and bloated. The puppy's ears should be pink and clean. Dark discharge or a bad odor could indicate ear mites, sure signs of poor maintenance. The healthy Chowlet's breath smells sweet. The teeth are clean and white and there should never be any malformation of the mouth or jaw. The puppy's dark eyes should be clear and bright and have that devilish little spark so typical of a Chow baby. Eyes that appear runny and irritated or eyes that are set so deep that the surrounding skin overlaps the pupil indicate serious problems.

There should be no sign of discharge from the nose, nor should the nose be crusted or runny. Coughing or diarrhea are danger signals, as are any eruptions on the skin. The puppy's coat should be soft and lustrous.

The healthy Chow puppy's legs should be as straight as little posts and the movement should be short and quick. The best way to describe Chow puppy movement is like that of a mechanical wind-up toy. Of course there is always a chubby clumsy puppy or two in a litter. Do not mistake this for unsoundness but if ever you have any doubts, discuss them with the breeder.

MALE OR FEMALE?

There are many breeds in which the sex makes little difference to the pet owner. I would not say this is so in the case of the Chow. While both the male and the female are capable of becoming excellent companions and are equally easy to housebreak, do consider the fact that a male Chow will mature to be considerably larger than his female littermates. He will weigh a great deal more and in most cases will have more coat to deal with. These are factors which should be taken into consideration as they will require more physical strength and greater maintenance time on the part of the owner.

There are other sex-related differences to consider as well. While the Chow is one of the cleanest and easiest breeds to housebreak, the male provides a problem in that respect which is sexually related. A male of any breed of dog has a natural instinct to lift his leg and "mark" his territory. The amount of effort that is involved in training the male not to do this varies with the individual dog, but what must be remembered is that a male considers everything in the household a part of his territory and he has an innate urge to establish this fact. This unfortunately may include your designer drapery or newly upholstered sofa.

Females, on the other hand, have their own set of problems. Females have their semi-annual heat cycles once they have reached eight or ten months of age. During these heat cycles of approximately 21 days, the female must be confined to avoid soiling her surroundings with the bloody discharge that accompanies estrus. She must also be carefully watched to prevent males from gaining access to her or she will become pregnant.

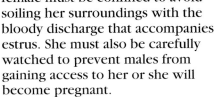

All of these lovable Chowlets want to be taken home, but as irresistible as they might be, make a careful and conscientious decision about which pup is right for you.

Both of these sexually related problems can be avoided by having the pet Chow "altered." Spaying the female and neutering the male saves the pet owner all the headaches of either of the sexually related problems without changing the character of the Chow. If there is any

change at all in the altered Chow, it is in making the dog an even more amiable companion. Above all, altering your pet precludes the possibility of its adding to the serious pet overpopulation problems that exist world-wide.

SELECTING A SHOW-QUALITY PUPPY

Should you be considering a show career for your Chow puppy, everything you have learned regarding soundness and health apply here as well. It must be remembered, though, that spaying and castration are not reversible procedures and, once done they eliminate the possibility of ever breeding or showing your Chow.

There are a good number of additional points to be considered for the show dog as well. First of all, it should be remembered that the most any breeder can offer is an opinion on the "show potential" of a particular puppy. The most promising eight-week-old puppy can grow up to be a mediocre adult. A breeder has no control over this.

Any predictions breeders make about a puppy's future are based upon their experience with past litters which have produced winning show dogs. It is obvious that the more successful a breeder has been in producing winning Chows over the years, the broader his base of comparison will be.

At five weeks old, it's too early to evaluate these puppies' show potential. Even if they do possess faults, they'll still make wonderful pets.

A puppy's potential as a show dog is determined by how closely it adheres to the demands of the standard of the breed. While most breeders concur that there is no such thing as "a sure thing" when it comes to predicting winners, they are also quick to agree that the older a puppy is, the better your chances are of making any predictions at all. If you are sincerely interested in showing your Chow, you

would do best to make your selection at about six months of age.

It makes little difference to the owner of a pet if his Chow has an off-color tongue or nose or if an ear hangs down a bit. Neither would it make a difference if a male pup had only one testicle. These faults do not interfere with a Chow becoming a healthy, loving companion. However, these flaws would keep that Chow from ever winning at a dog show.

It certainly behooves the prospective buyer of a show-quality puppy to be as familiar with the standard of the breed as possible. It is also highly advisable for the buyer to put himself into the hands of a successful and respected breeder of winning Chows. The experienced breeder knows that there are certain age-related shortcomings in young Chows that maturity will

When selecting a dog for show, you must not be swayed by "cuteness" alone. Adorable though they may be, you must seriously consider the puppy's conformation.

take care of and other faults that completely eliminate the dog from consideration as a show prospect. Also, breeders are always looking for the right homes in which to place their show-quality puppies and will be particularly helpful when they know that you plan to show one of their dogs.

The important thing to remember in choosing your first show prospect is that "cuteness" may not be consistent with quality. An extroverted puppy in the litter might decide it belongs to you. If you are simply looking for a pet, that is the Chow for you. However, if you are genuinely interested in showing your Chow, you must keep your head. Without disregarding good temperament, give serious consideration to what the standard says a show type Chow must be.

Look for the pup in a litter that looks like a little box, measuring the same from forechest to rump as it does from the top of the shoulders to the ground. His tail should be carried up and on the back. The Chow is a "square" breed. Any puppy that appears short on its legs or long in its body should not be considered at all for the show ring. The overall impression is of a little tank—broad in front and chunky from one end to the other.

There are only five true Chow colors but there are an endless range of shadings of those five colors and these change drastically between puppyhood and full maturity. The five colors are: red, black, blue, cinnamon and cream.

Choose a puppy with strong straight gun-barrel legs, with the rear legs appearing nearly as straight as those in front. A spindly looking pup is all wrong for a Chow.

The Chow puppy's head appears large for its body. A strong square head with a broad deep muzzle is typical of the good Chow. Very dark eyes are a must and they must be small and triangular looking. The pigment of the inside of the mouth and lips should definitely be black, and don't forget that the top of a show-quality Chow's tongue can only be black or blue-black. The nose must be black as well unless you are looking at what is called a blue Chow, which is simply a dilution of the color black. In that case, the nose is allowed to be blue or slate-colored. The ears are small, stiff and erect.

You have a choice of coats. That decision depends totally upon your personal preference.

These are the obvious characteristics of a Chow puppy with show potential. There are many nuances of breed type that are best understood by an experienced breeder of show-quality Chows. Rely upon someone who has had this experience to assist you in selecting a puppy of promise. There is an old breeders saying that applies well here. "Breed the best to the best. Select the best and then hope for the best!"

ADOPTING AN ADULT

A young puppy is not your only option when contemplating the purchase of a Chow. In some cases an adult dog may be just the answer. It certainly eliminates the trials and tribulations of housebreaking, chewing and the myriad of other problems associated with a young puppy. In the case of Chows, however, the decision to bring an adult dog into the home must be carefully considered.

The adult Chow will invariably be very set in its ways and this is not, as we have mentioned previously, a breed that easily changes its mind. An adult Chow will be accustomed to being treated in a particular way. If the treatment was kind and loving, the adult Chow will expect that to continue and will respond accordingly. If the Chow was improperly socialized or was mistreated, there is every reason to believe that the adult is going to be wary of humans in general and strangers in particular. Chows that have not been raised with children may well be shocked at their initial introduction to these "miniature people" and respond with fear and protectiveness.

If you decide to adopt an adult Chow, be aware that he may possess habits that do not fit into your lifestyle.

All this said, an adult Chow that came from a kind and loving home could be the perfect answer for the elderly or someone who is forced to be away from home during the day. While it would be unreasonable to expect a young puppy not to relieve itself in the house if you are gone many hours, it would be surprising to find a Chow who in adulthood would even consider relieving itself in the home in which it lives.

Chows do become set in their ways and while you may not have to contend with the problems of puppyhood, do realize that the adult might have developed habits that do not suit you or your lifestyle. My best advice is to carefully consider the advantages and drawbacks of adding an adult Chow to your household. Should you decide to do so, arrange that it be done initially on a trial basis. That way neither you nor the Chow will be obligated should either of you decide you are incompatible.

IDENTIFICATION PAPERS

The purchase of any purebred dog entitles you to three very important documents: a health certificate containing an inoculation record, a copy of the dog's pedigree and the dog's registration certificate.

Most Chow breeders have initiated the necessary inoculation series for their puppies by the time they are eight weeks of age. These inoculations protect the puppies against hepatitis, leptospirosis, distemper and canine parvovirus. In most cases, rabies inoculations are not given until a puppy is six months of age or older.

There is a set series of inoculations developed to combat these infectious diseases and it is extremely important that you obtain a record of the shots your puppy has been given and the dates upon which the shots were administered. This way, the veterinarian you choose will be able to continue on with the appropriate inoculation series as needed.

The pedigree is your dog's "family tree." The breeder must supply you with a copy of this document authenticating your puppy's ancestors back to at least the third generation.

The registration certificate is the canine world's "birth certificate." This certificate is issued by a country's governing kennel club. When you transfer the ownership of your Chow from the breeder's name to your own name, the transaction is entered on this certificate. Once it is mailed to the kennel club, it is permanently recorded in their computerized files. Keep all of these documents in a safe place, as you will need them when you visit your veterinarian or should you ever wish to breed or show your Chow.

DIET SHEET

Your Chowlet is a happy healthy puppy because the breeder has been carefully feeding and caring for it. Every breeder we know has his own particular way of doing this. Most breeders give the new owner a written record that details the amount and kind of food a puppy has been receiving. Follow these recommendations to the letter at least for the first month or two after the puppy comes to live with you.

The diet sheet should indicate the number of times a day your Chow has been accustomed to being fed and the kind of vitamin supplementation, if any, it has been receiving. Following the prescribed procedure will reduce the chance of upset stomach and loose stools.

Usually a breeder's diet sheet projects the increases and changes in food that will be necessary as your puppy grows from week to week. If the sheet does not include this information, ask the breeder for suggestions regarding increases and the eventual changeover to adult food.

In the unlikely event you are not supplied with a diet sheet by the breeder and are unable to get one, your veterinarian will be able to advise you in this respect. There are countless foods now being manufactured expressly to meet the nutritional needs of puppies and growing dogs. A trip down the pet aisle at your supermarket will prove just how many choices you have. Two important tips to remember: read labels carefully for content. When dealing with established reliable manufacturers, you are more likely to get what you pay for.

HEALTH GUARANTEE

Any reputable breeder is more than willing to supply a written agreement that the sale of your Chow is contingent upon its passing a veterinarian's examination. Ideally you will be able to arrange an appointment with your chosen veterinarian right after you have picked up your puppy from the breeder and before you take the puppy home. If this is not possible, you should not delay

Reputable breeders will have started their Chow puppies on the road to good nutrition, so stick faithfully to a healthy diet and make any changes very gradually.

this procedure any longer than 24 hours from the time you take your puppy home.

TEMPERAMENT AND SOCIALIZATION

Temperament is both hereditary and learned. Inherited good temperament can be ruined by poor treatment and lack of proper socialization. A Chow puppy that has inherited a bad temperament is a poor risk as either a companion or show dog and should certainly never be bred. Therefore, it is critical that you obtain a happy puppy from a breeder who is determined to produce good temperaments and who has taken all the necessary steps to provide the much-needed early socialization.

It is important that Chow puppies socialize with their littermates. These two six and a half-week-old buddies obviously have a playful relationship!

Temperaments in the same litter can range from strong-willed and outgoing on the high end of the scale to shy and fearful at the low end. A puppy that is so bold and strong-willed as to be foolhardy and uncontrollable could easily be a difficult adult that needs a very firm hand. This is hardly a dog for the owner who is mild and reserved in demeanor or frail in physique. In every human-canine relationship there must be a pack leader and a follower. The dominant alpha-type Chow must have an owner who remains in charge at all times or the dog itself will assume command.

On the opposite end of the scale is the Chow that is shy and fearful. This is not a dog that should be considered as a household companion nor should it ever be bred. Fear biters can be among the most dangerous of dogs for often there seems to be no apparent rhyme or reason to their biting. This is a dog that should be dealt with only by the most experienced of trainers and even then the temperament is never totally reliable.

Fortunately, most Chows today fall into the middle to high temperament range, which produces an dog that is outgoing yet calm and responsive enough to be easily trained. This is the puppy that makes the best companion and show dog. Still, it is important to remember that a Chow puppy may be happy living at home with you and your family, but if the socialization begun by the breeder is not continued, that sunny disposition will not extend outside your front door. From the day the

Every person who visits your house should be encouraged to hold and pet your Chow. It is not hard to persuade your guests to play with your little "teddy bear!"

young Chow arrives at your home, you must be committed to accompanying it on an unending pilgrimage to meet and befriend all types of human beings and animals.

If you are fortunate enough to have children in the household or living nearby, your socialization task will be assisted considerably. Chows raised with children are the best. The two seem to understand each other in some way known only to the puppies and children themselves; they give each other the confidence to face the trying ordeal of growing up.

The children in your own household are not the only children your Chowlet should spend time with. It is a case of the more the merrier! Every child (and adult for that matter) that enters your household should be asked to hold and pet your Chow puppy.

If trustworthy neighborhood children live nearby, have them take the puppy on short walks. If there is adult supervision, an afternoon visit to the children's home is a grand idea!

Your puppy should go everywhere with you: the post office, the market, to the shopping mall—wherever. Be prepared to create a stir wherever you go because the very reason that attracted you to the first Chowlet you met applies here as well. Everyone will want to pet your little "teddy bear" and there is nothing in the world better for him.

Chows who will be shown must be amenable to handling and must accept examination by a judge. These pups practice standing still—for puppies, that's the hardest part!

Should your puppy back off from a stranger, pick him up and hand him to the person. You must insist that your young Chow be amenable to the attention of all strangers— young and old, short and tall, and of all races. It is not up to your puppy to decide who it will or will not be friendly with. You are in charge. You must call the shots.

If your Chow has a show career in its future, there are other things in addition to just being handled that will have to be taught. All Chow show dogs must learn to have their mouths opened and inspected by the judge. The judge must be able to check the teeth and see if the tongue is a solid blue-black color. Males must be accustomed to having their testicles touched as the dog show judge must determine that all male dogs are "complete," which means there are two normal-sized testicles in the scrotum. These inspections must begin in puppyhood and be done on a regular and continuing basis.

All Chows must learn to get on with other dogs as well as with humans. If you are fortunate enough to have a dog park nearby, visit it with your puppy as frequently as possible, daily if time permits. A young Chow that has been exposed regularly to other dogs from puppyhood will learn to adapt and accept other dogs and other breeds much more readily than a Chow that seldom sees strange dogs.

CARING for Your Chow Chow

You will find it amazing how quickly the little ball of fur you first brought home begins to develop into a full-grown Chow. Some lines shoot up to full size very rapidly, others mature more slowly. Some dogs pass through adolescence quite gracefully while others become clumsy and ungainly and grow in and out of proportion, seemingly from one day to the next. Somewhere between 12–18 months, your Chow will have attained its full height. However, body and coat development continue on until two years of age in some lines and up to three or four in others. Food needs to be increased during this growth period. Some dogs seem as if they can never get enough to eat while others eat just enough to avoid starving. Think of puppies as being as individualistic as children and act accordingly.

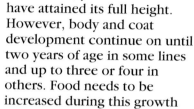

Your Chow puppy's food intake needs to be increased during his growth periods. Each puppy is an individual, however, so adjust your Chow's diet accordingly.

All Chows pass through a period when the puppy coat is shed and the adult coat is beginning to come in. It is essential that you give grooming all the attention it requires at this time to remove the dead puppy hair so the new coat can come through easily. If not regularly brushed during this period, the coat mats quickly and will require extreme corrective measures.

This adolescent period is a particularly important one. It is the time your Chow must learn all the household and social rules by which it will live for the rest of its life. Your patience and commitment during this time will not only produce a respected canine good citizen but will also forge a bond

Good nutrition will show in your Chow's healthy, shiny coat and bright, clear eyes. A balanced diet will make all the difference in appearance of your dog.

between the two of you that will grow and ripen into a wonderful relationship.

FEEDING AND NUTRITION

The best way to make sure your Chow puppy is obtaining the right amount and the correct type of food for its age is to follow the diet sheet provided by the breeder from whom you obtain your puppy. Do not change the puppy's diet and you will be less apt to run into digestive problems and diarrhea. Diarrhea is very serious in young puppies. Puppies with diarrhea can dehydrate very rapidly, causing severe problems and even death.

If it is necessary to change your Chow's diet for any reason, it should be done gradually, over a period of several meals and a few days. Begin by adding a tablespoon or two of the new food, gradually increasing the amount until the meal consists entirely of the new product.

By the time your Chow is 12 months old, you can reduce the frequency of feedings to once a day. This meal can be given either in the morning or evening. It is really a matter of choice on your part. There are two important things to remember: feed the main meal at the same time every day and make sure that what you feed is nutritionally complete.

The single meal can be supplemented by a morning or night time snack of hard dog biscuits, such as Chooz™ by Nylabone®, made especially for large dogs. These biscuits not only become highly anticipated treats by your Chow but are genuinely helpful in maintaining healthy gums and teeth.

"BALANCED" DIETS

In order for a canine diet to qualify as "complete and balanced" in the United States, it must meet standards set by the Subcommittee on Canine Nutrition of the National Research Council of the National Academy of Sciences. Most commercial foods manufactured for dogs meet these standards and prove this by listing the ingredients contained in the food on every package and can. The ingredients are listed in descending order with the main ingredient listed first.

Fed with any regularity at all, refined sugars can cause your Chow to become obese and will definitely create tooth decay. Candy stores do not exist in the wild and canine teeth are not genetically disposed to handling sugars. Do not feed your

Newborn puppies get the important vitamins and minerals they need from nursing. Once they are weaned, the owner must fulfill their nutritional requirements.

Chow sugar products and avoid products that contain sugar to any high degree.

Fresh water and a properly prepared, balanced diet containing the essential nutrients in correct proportions are all that a healthy Chow needs to be offered. Dog foods come canned, dry, semi-moist, "scientifically fortified" and "all-natural." A visit to your local supermarket or pet store will reveal how vast an array you will be able to select from.

The wide variety of Nylabone® products will provide your Chow puppy with hours of entertainment while strengthening his teeth and jaw.

The important thing to remember, however, is that all dogs, whether they are Chows or Chihuahuas, are carnivorous (meat-eating) animals. While the vegetable content of your Chow's diet should not be overlooked, a dog's physiology and anatomy are based upon carnivorous food acquisition. Protein and fat are absolutely essential to the well-being of your Chow. In fact, it is wise to add a tablespoon or two of vegetable oil or bacon drippings to your dog's diet, particularly during winter months.

Read the list of ingredients on the dog food you buy. Animal protein should appear first on the label's list of ingredients. A base of quality kibble to which the meat and even table scraps have been added can provide a nutritious meal for your Chow.

This having been said, it should be realized that in the wild carnivores eat the entire beast they that capture and kill. The carnivore's kills consist almost entirely of herbivores (plant eating animals) and invariably the carnivore begins its meal with the contents of the herbivore's stomach. This provides the carbohydrates, minerals and nutrients present in vegetables.

Through centuries of domestication we have made our dogs entirely dependent upon us for their well-being. Therefore we are entirely responsible for duplicating the food balance that the wild dog finds in nature. The domesticated dog's diet must include protein, carbohydrates, fats, roughage and small amounts of essential minerals and vitamins.

Finding commercially prepared diets that contain all of the necessary nutrients will not present a problem. It is important to understand, though, that these commercially prepared foods do contain all the necessary nutrients your Chow needs. It is therefore unnecessary to add vitamin supplements to these diets in other than special circumstances prescribed by your veterinarian. Over-supplementation and forced growth are now looked upon by some breeders as major contributors to many skeletal abnormalities found in the purebred dogs of the day.

Over-Supplementation

A great deal of controversy exists today regarding the orthopedic problems such as hip, elbow and patella (knee) dysplasia that afflict Chows and many other breeds. Some claim that these problems are entirely hereditary conditions but many others feel that they can be exacerbated by the over-use of mineral and vitamin supplements for puppies.

In giving vitamin supplementation, one should never exceed the prescribed amount. Some breeders insist that all recommended dosages be halved before including them in a dog's diet. Still other breeders feel that no supplementation should be given at all, believing a balanced diet that includes plenty of milk products and a small amount of bone meal to provide calcium is all that is necessary and beneficial.

Pregnant and lactating bitches may require supplementation of some kind but here again it is not a case of "if a little is good, a lot would be a great deal better." Extreme caution is advised in this case and best discussed with your veterinarian.

If the owner of a Chow normally eats healthy nutritious food, there is no reason why his dog can not be given table scraps. What could possibly be harmful in good nutritious food?

Table scraps should be given only as part of the dog's meal and never from the table. A Chow that becomes accustomed to being hand fed from the table can quickly become a real pest at meal time. Also, dinner guests may find the pleading stare of your Chow less than appealing when dinner is being served.

Dogs do not care if food looks like a hot dog or wedge of cheese. Truly nutritious dog foods are seldom manufactured to look like food that appeals to humans. Dogs only care about how food smells and tastes. It is highly doubtful that you will be eating your dog's food, so do not waste your money on these "looks just like" products.

Along these lines, most of the moist foods or canned foods that have the look of "delicious red beef" look that way because they contain great amounts of preservatives and dyes. Preservatives and dyes are no better for your dog than they are for you.

You should only supplement your Chow's diet if it has been recommended by your veterinarian, and then be sure to never exceed the prescribed amount.

Special Diets

There are now any number of commercially prepared diets for dogs with special dietary needs. The overweight, underweight or geriatric dog can have its nutritional needs met as can puppies and growing dogs. The calorie content of these foods is adjusted accordingly. With the correct amount of the right foods and the proper amount of exercise, your Chow should stay in top shape. Again, common sense must prevail. Too many calories will increase weight, too few will reduce weight.

Occasionally a young Chow going through the teething period will become a poor eater. The concerned owner's first response is to tempt the dog by hand-feeding special treats and foods that the problem eater seems to prefer. This practice only serves to compound the problem. Once the dog learns to play the waiting game, it will turn up its nose at anything other than its favorite food knowing full well that what it wants to eat will eventually arrive.

Unlike humans, dogs have no suicidal tendencies. A healthy dog will not starve itself to death. It may not eat enough to keep itself in the shape we find ideal and attractive, but it will definitely eat enough to maintain itself. If your Chow is not eating properly and appears to be too thin, it is probably best to consult your veterinarian

BATHING AND GROOMING

It is important to remember that the Chow is a natural breed that requires no clipping or trimming outside of tidying up its feet or removing its whiskers. Breeders are most adamant that the Chow not fall into any grooming fads of any kind. Proper brushing is all the grooming that your Chow will ever need.

Puppy Coat

Undoubtedly the breeder from whom you purchased your Chowlet began to accustom the puppy to grooming just as soon as there was enough hair to brush. You must continue on with grooming sessions or begin them at once if for some reason they have not been started. You and your Chow will spend many hours involved with this activity over a lifetime, so it is imperative that both of you learn to cooperate in the endeavor to make it an easy and pleasant experience.

Your puppy should become accustomed to being groomed at a very young age. Once your Chow gets used to it, it will be a pleasant experience for both of you.

The first piece of equipment you will have to obtain is a grooming table. A grooming table can be built or purchased at your local pet store. Even a sturdy card table topped with a non-skid pad will suffice. Make

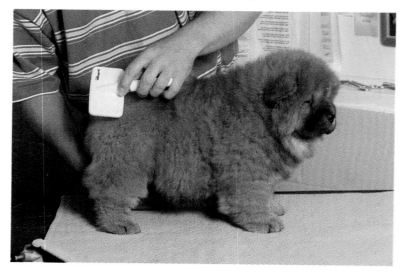

Use a grooming table when working on your Chow Chow's coat. He will not be able to run away from you, and you will be able to do the job thoroughly.

sure the table is of a height at which you can work comfortably either sitting or standing. Adjustable-height grooming tables are available at most pet shops. Although you will buy this when your Chow puppy first arrives, anticipate its full grown size in making your purchase and select or build a table that will accommodate a fully grown Chow lying on its side.

You will also need to invest in two brushes, a steel comb, barber's scissors, and a pair of nail clippers. For the finish work you will need a commercial coat conditioner and a spray bottle. Consider the fact that you will be using this equipment for many years, so buy the best of these items that you can afford.

The two brushes that you will need are a wire slicker brush (also called a rake) and a pin brush (sometimes called a Poodle brush).

Do not attempt to groom your Chow on the floor. The puppy will only attempt to get away from you when it has decided enough is enough, and you will spend a good part of your time chasing the puppy around the room. Additionally, sitting on the floor for long stretches of time is not the most comfortable position in the world for the average adult.

The Chow puppy must be taught to lie on its side to be groomed. It will be kept in that position for most of the grooming process. The puppy will also have to be kept in the sitting and standing positions but the lying position takes the most time and is more difficult for the puppy to learn. The Chow trained to lie quietly on its side will prove to be a true godsend when the dog is fully grown and has developed a mature coat.

Begin this training by picking the puppy up with its side against your chest and your arms wrapped around the puppy's body. Lay the puppy down on the table and release your arms but keep your chest pressed lightly down on the puppy's side. Speak reassuringly to the Chowlet, stroking its head and rump. (This is a good time to practice the "stay" command.) Do this a number of times before you attempt to do any grooming. Repeat the process until your puppy understands what it is supposed to do when you place it on the grooming table.

Start with the slicker brush and begin what is called line brushing at the top of the shoulder. Part the hair in a straight line from the front of the shoulder straight on down to the bottom of the chest. Brush through the hair to the right and left of the part, lightly spraying the area with the coat conditioner as you go. Start at the skin and brush out to the very end of the hair. Do a small section at a time and continue on down the part. When you reach the bottom of the part, return to the top and make another part just to the right of the first line you brushed. Part, brush and spray. You will repeat this process working toward the rear until you reach the puppy's tail.

I prefer to do the legs on the same side I have been working on at this time. Use the same process, parting the hair at

You can use barber's scissors to trim any long hair at your Chow's feet and to trim his whiskers. However some owners prefer to leave the whiskers alone.

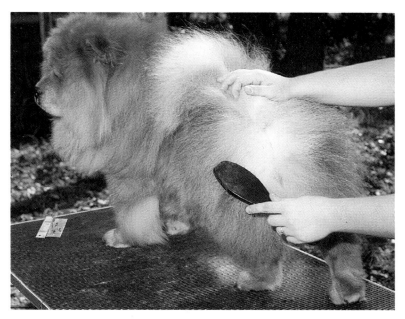

When grooming, part your Chow's hair at the top of each leg and work your way down to the feet. Don't forget to brush those hard-to-reach areas where mats can occur.

the top of the leg and working down. Do this all around the leg and be especially careful to attend to the hard-to-reach areas under the upper legs where they join the body. Mats occur in these areas very rapidly, especially during the time when the Chow is shedding its puppy coat.

Should you encounter a mat that does not brush out easily, use your fingers and the steel comb to separate the hairs as much as possible. Do not cut or pull out the matted hair. Apply baby powder or one of the specially prepared grooming powders directly to the mat and brush completely from the skin out.

When you have finished the legs on the one side, turn the puppy over and complete the entire process on the other side—part, spray, brush. As your Chowlet becomes accustomed to this process you may find that the puppy considers this nap time. You may have to lift your puppy into sitting position to arouse it from its slumber.

While the puppy is sitting, you can do the hair on the chest using the line brushing method here as well. Next, stand the puppy up and do the tail. Check the longer hair of the "pants" on the rear legs to make sure they are thoroughly brushed, especially around the area of the anus and genitalia. Needless to say, it is important to be extremely careful when brushing in these areas in that they are extremely sensitive and easily injured.

When the line brushing process is completed, it is time for the finishing touches. Use your barber's scissors to trim any long or shaggy hairs around the Chow's feet—his feet should be round and compact looking. You may trim off your Chow's whiskers if you wish. This is optional, however. Many Chow owners prefer to leave the whiskers on.

Because the nails of a Chow are black, it can be difficult to determine where to cut. Let your veterinarian show you how.

Brush the hair around the head, the shoulders and the back forward. Do the same with the hair on the tail. Brush the chest hair downward and do the same with the hair on the sides of the dog.

This is a good time to accustom your Chow to having its nails trimmed and having its feet inspected. Always inspect your dog's feet for cracked pads. Check between the toes for splinters and thorns. Pay particular attention to any swollen or tender areas. In many sections of the country, there is a weed that has a barbed "hook" that carries its seed. This hook can easily find its way into a Chow's foot or between its toes and can work its way deep into the dog's flesh very quickly, causing soreness and infection. These barbs are best removed by your veterinarian before serious problems result.

The nails of a Chow who spends most of its time indoors or on grass when outdoors can grow long very quickly. Do not allow the nails to become overgrown and then expect to cut them back easily. Each nail has a blood vessel running through its center called the quick. The quick grows close to the end of the nail and contains very sensitive nerve endings. If the nail is allowed to grow too long it will be impossible to cut it back to a proper length without cutting into the quick. This causes severe pain to the dog and can also result in a great deal of bleeding that can be very difficult to stop.

If your Chow is getting plenty of exercise on cement or rough hard pavement, the nails may keep sufficiently worn down. Otherwise, the nails can grow long very quickly. They must then be trimmed with canine nail clippers, an electric nail grinder (also called a drummel) or a coarse file made expressly for canine nails. All three of these items can be purchased at any pet store.

We prefer the electric nail grinder because it is so easy to control and helps avoid cutting into the quick. The Chow's dark nails make it practically impossible to see where the quick ends, so regardless of which nail trimming device is used, one must proceed with caution and remove only a small portion of the nail at a time.

Use of the electric grinder requires introducing your puppy to it at an early age. The instrument has a whining sound to it not unlike a dentist's drill. The noise combined with the vibration of the sanding head on the nail can take some getting used to, but most dogs I have used it on eventually accept it as one of life's trials. Most dogs do not like having their nails trimmed no matter which device is used, so my own eventual decision was to use the grinder as I was less apt to damage the quick.

Should the quick be nipped in the trimming process, there are any number of blood-clotting products available at pet shops that will almost immediately stem the flow of blood. It is wise to have one of these products on hand in case there is a nail trimming accident or the dog tears a nail on its own.

Grooming the Adult Chow

Fortunately, you and your Chow have spent the many months between puppyhood and full maturity learning to assist each other through the grooming process. The two of you have survived the shedding of the puppy coat and the arrival of the entirely different adult hair. Not only is the Chow's adult hair of an entirely different texture, it is much longer and much thicker.

Undoubtedly by this time you have realized that the pin brush, with its longer bristles set in rubber, is far more effective for line brushing the adult Chow than the slicker brush that you used through puppyhood. The method of brushing the adult coat is the same as that of brushing the puppy coat. The difference is more dog and more hair.

While one might expect grooming an adult Chow to be a monumental task, this is not necessarily so. The two of you have been practicing the brushing routine for so long that it has undoubtedly become second nature to both of you. The coarseness of the adult Chow's hair is actually much easier to cope with than the hair of the puppy coat. The ease of working with the Chow's adult coat plus your own experience with the grooming routine combine to make the task far easier than what one might expect. Ten industriously applied minutes a day with a brush plus a thorough weekly session will keep your Chow looking in the best of shape.

You may think that the Chow's heavy coat is too warm in the summer, but it actually acts as insulation from both heat and cold. This guy is well protected from any element.

On the other hand, if the coat is neglected and becomes matted, you will indeed have a difficult time ahead of you. The coat can become felted with mats and you may have to resort to having a veterinarian or groomer shave the matted-to-the-skin Chow. This should be resorted to only under extreme circumstances. Some misguided owners feel that they are doing their dogs a service by shaving their coats in summer when exactly the opposite is true. The Chow's coat serves as insulation against both heat and cold.

Bathing

Following the foregoing coat care procedure will all but eliminate the need for bathing a Chow. Dog show exhibitors use coat care products that adhere to the Chow's hair and may make bathing necessary on occasion. Even then, most Chow exhibitors use dry bath products rather than the tub and shampoo method. Well-kept Chows are literally odor free and frequent bathing serves little purpose. Bathing can dry out the Chow's skin and hair, creating unnecessary problems.

If you must bathe your Chow, never bathe it while matted. Wetting the matted hair will only complicate the situation and the end result will provide you with much more work than if you had completed the mat removal process prior to bathing. On the rare occasions that your Chow requires a wet bath, you will need to gather the necessary equipment ahead of time.

A rubber mat should be placed at the bottom of the tub to avoid your Chow slipping and thereby becoming frightened. A rubber spray hose is absolutely necessary to thoroughly wet the Chow's dense coat. The hose is also necessary to remove all shampoo residue.

A steel comb is helpful for separating mats, as well as for putting the finishing touches on your Chow's coat.

A small cotton ball placed inside each ear will keep water from running down into the dog's ear canal and a drop or two of mineral oil or a dab of petroleum jelly placed in each eye will preclude shampoo irritating the Chow's eyes.

It is best to use a shampoo designed especially for dogs. The pH balance is adjusted to keep drying to a minimum and to leave the hair shining and lustrous.

In bathing, start behind the ears and work back. Use a wash cloth to soap and rinse around the head and face. Once you have shampooed your Chow, you must rinse the coat thoroughly. When you feel quite certain that all shampoo residue has been removed, rinse once more. Shampoo residue in the coat is sure to dry the hair and could cause skin irritation.

As soon as you have completed the bath, use heavy towels to remove as much of the excess water as possible. Your Chow will assist you in the process by shaking a great deal of the water out of its coat on its own.

Before your Chow is completely dry it is best to brush out the coat to prevent mats and tangles from forming. Use the same brushing process you normally use.

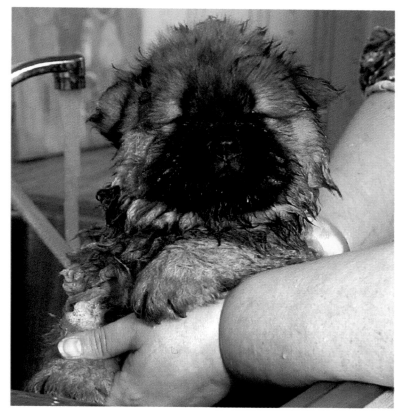

If his coat is well cared for, your Chow will rarely require a wet bath. When he does, be sure to use a shampoo designed especially for dogs.

My advice is to avoid the wet bath unless it is absolutely necessary. There are so many effective dry bath products available that the time consuming wet bath need only be resorted to in extreme circumstances.

EXERCISE

If your own exercise proclivities lie closer to the couch than to the Iron Man Triathlon, choosing a Chow as your companion was probably a smart idea. The Chow is one breed that does not require its owner to be a cross-country runner or mountain climber. A good brisk walk around a few of the neighborhood blocks will keep both you and your pal alive and breathing. More blocks more often will, of course, keep you both alive and breathing for a much longer time.

Most Chows will willingly walk as far as, and perhaps further than, their owners are inclined to go. Daily walks combined with some ball retrieving or game playing in the yard can keep the average Chow in fine fettle. If your Chow is fortunate enough to share its life with another dog or with children, exercise will not be a problem. Contrary to their dignified expression, Chows love to romp and play and will attempt to entice the people or animals they like to join them.

Hot Weather

Caution must be exercised in hot weather. The Chow is a short-muzzled breed that should not be forced to exercise when temperatures are high. Plan your walks for the first thing in the morning if at all possible. If this does not work into your schedule, wait until evening after the sun has gone down.

You must never leave your Chow in a car in hot weather. Temperatures can soar in a matter of minutes and Chows are unable to cope with the resulting heat even briefly. Rolling down the windows helps little and is dangerous in that an over-heated Chow will attempt to escape in panic. Chows are very susceptible to heat stroke and can die within minutes if you are not continually vigilant. A word to the wise—leave your Chow at home in a cool room on hot days.

Cold weather and even temperatures hovering around the zero mark are no problem at all for the Chow. The only warm clothing required will be yours.

Special Needs

Socialization

Unlike a good number of other breeds, the Chow is not a needy or dependent dog. The breed is incredibly independent and as long as the person or persons it loves are nearby, the Chow is completely happy. In fact, the Chow would be just as happy if there were no others, human or animal, to interfere with its happy personal world.

On the surface this might appear to be just fine but as the saying goes, "No man (or dog!) is an island." In today's urban society, humans and canines must be able to get on with their neighbors. It is up to you to insist through proper training that your Chow understands and adapts to this social rule.

Independent Nature

Most Chow owners find that the breed is one that can entertain itself for long periods of time. Our Blossom invested hours on end working on her "butterfly collection." Blossom loved to chase the countless butterflies that for some unknown reason found our garden the most attractive in the neighborhood. Occasionally she actually captured one of her "winged monsters" and surprised herself as much as she did us.

Blossom also invented games of hide-and-seek, never catching on to the fact that hiding only her head did not in fact keep her out of sight. When we called, she would remain "hidden" with her tail wagging furiously, obviously quite proud of her ability to conceal herself from her owners.

Some people thoroughly enjoy dog training, the more complex and demanding the lessons are, the better. There are many breeds that are not only adept at these lessons, they actually thrive on being put through the paces and become difficult if not required to perform.

You must be cautious about your Chow's health in hot weather. Do not leave him outside for long periods of time and make sure he always has cool clean water to drink.

73

Your Chow will crave the security of his own "den." A crate will provide your dog with unlimited access to his own private space.

This is not necessarily so of the Chow. Its independent but loving nature make the breed trainable, but it is not necessary to spend hours on end inventing activities designed to keep an adult Chow out of mischief. The Chow is a dog more suited to the independent, free-of-spirit human who has no particular need to be surrounded by automatons waiting to leap to the next command.

Private Retreat

The Chow enjoys having a special place of his own in the household. This is a "cave" or "den" they can retreat to in order to think things out or to store their special treasures. The best way to provide your Chow with this retreat is by providing it with a crate placed in some out of the way corner. Crates can be made of fiberglass, such as the type used by the airlines for shipping dogs, or they can be made of metal wire.

The metal wire crates are ideal for the Chow. They provide good air circulation and, if necessary, can be covered to keep out drafts. These wire crates are normally collapsible for easy transportation when traveling. Throwing a dark-colored piece of material over the top of the crate provides a cave-like atmosphere but does not block out air circulation.

You will be amazed at how attached your Chow will become to its "cave." It provides a sense of security, as dogs are inclined to select a place where they can sleep under or against something. The crate will provide your Chow with constant access to a place of this kind.

THE CHOW AND OTHER PETS

We know of Chows whose best friends (after their owners) are cats. This is not entirely surprising in that there is a bit of the cat in the Chow itself. But this is a relationship that should be established early on, while the pair is still in the kitten and puppy stage. A Chow puppy is apt to be a bit rough and tumble for the average kitten, but on the other hand, kittens compensate for their lack of brute strength with flexibility and maneuverability that can leave the less agile Chow puppy wondering what happened!

A well-cared for Chow will look healthy and be eager to please his master.

Chows are really at their best in one-dog households. Raising a Chow with another dog creates the possibility of your Chow's bonding more closely to its canine partner rather than to you. Should you want your Chow to share you and your household with another dog, it is best for the pair be of opposite sexes. This is especially so if both are Chows. Fights are bound to occur between Chows and even other breeds of the same sex, and once a Chow has a fight it is highly unlikely the fight will ever be forgotten. This is a dangerous and volatile situation that is best avoided.

Chows are not usually inclined to pick fights with other breeds, but for some reason, dogs of other more aggressive breeds seem to have an inclination to pick fights with Chows. It has been said that other breeds react to the Chow's distinctive odor. Regardless, if attacked, the Chow will fight to defend itself and will fight to the death if need be. You will find that when pressed, the Chow has not forgotten its war dog heritage.

Should you wish to have a two-dog household, some careful thought ahead of time can avoid problems. First, it is easier to bring a Chow puppy into a mature dog's household, especially if the older dog is of the opposite sex and of an amiable disposition. An adult Chow is not going to be particularly thrilled to

Chows thrive in one-dog households. If you are planning to introduce another pet into your home, it is easier to add a puppy to a mature dog's territory.

Because the Chow's legs lack flexibility, it is very dangerous to drop your dog to the ground after holding him. Remember to always lower him gently from high places.

have its home turf invaded by a puppy and might be rough in showing its displeasure if not properly supervised.

Regardless of age, some thought should be given to compatibility. When the choice can be made, it would be wise to choose one of the more passive breeds to share a Chow's household. Bringing in another breed with as dominant a personality as the Chow's can only lead to problems.

CARE OF THE CHOW'S LEGS

It is very important to remember not to drop your Chow puppy to the ground after you have picked it up. Because of the construction of the Chow's legs, particularly its back legs, it does not have the flexibility of most other breeds. Imagine yourself jumping off a high ladder and landing without flexing your knees and it will give you an idea of what this sudden impact will do to a Chow puppy or worse, to an adult. Make sure you lower your Chow to the ground when it has been up on the grooming table or if you have it in your arms.

In addition, it is best to keep your Chow at the low end of its ideal weight range rather than allowing it to become overweight. Excess weight takes its toll on your Chow's legs and can cause serious problems. Pushing your puppy's growth rate and over-feeding can seriously impair your dog's orthopedic welfare.

HOUSEBREAKING and Training

There is no breed of dog that cannot be trained. Some breeds appear to be more difficult to get the desired response from than others. This is more apt to be due to the trainer not being breed specific in his or her approach to the training than the dog's inability to learn. With the proper approach, any dog that is not mentally deficient can be taught to be a good canine citizen.

Ease of training depends greatly upon just how much a dog depends upon its master's approval. The entirely dependent dog lives to please its master and will do everything in its power to evoke the approval response from the person it is devoted to.

At the opposite end of the pole we have the totally independent dog who is not remotely concerned with what its master thinks. Dependency varies from one breed to the next and within breeds as well. Chows are no exception to this rule. One thing you will never have to be concerned with in any Chow is having it become overly dependent! Successfully training a Chow depends upon your fully understanding the breed's character and dealing with it accordingly.

Some professionals who train dogs advise obtaining a puppy on the 49th day of its life. Their research indicates it is at this precise point in time that a puppy is most ready to bond to a human and subsequently depend upon that person for approval. Prior to that time, the puppy needs to be with its siblings and mother. Just after the 49th day, the puppy passes through various stages that make it less ideal for human bonding and more independent in nature.

Not all behaviorists will ascribe to the 49th day theory but there does seem to be general agreement that the optimum time to bring a puppy into its new home is at about 7–8 weeks of age. It is wise to at least consider this information and discuss it with the breeder from whom you will be purchasing your puppy.

The average Chow is not as easily won over by verbal praise as other more dependent breeds. Your Chow is far more apt to be motivated by a food treat than by telling it what a wonderful dog it is.

The biggest problem in our loving but fiercely independent Chow is off-leash response. The dependent dog has a natural inclination to stay near to its owner. The independent Chow has a lot on its mind that it wants to attend to and is not particularly concerned if its human companion is of the same mind.

Because of his independent nature, the Chow may tend to wander away. When he's off his leash, be sure keep your Chow in a fenced-in area at all times

This lack of concern on your Chow's part is extremely important to remember. As devoted a companion as your Chow might be and as much as you may love it, never allow your Chow to be off leash when you are out of the confines of your home and yard!

Do not confuse the Chow's independence with being untrustworthy. This is not the case at all. It has little to do with trust and much to do with the breed's belief that it can fend for itself. Keeping all this in mind will make your approach to training a much easier task than having expectations of your Chow which the dog will find extremely difficult, if not impossible, to live up to.

Your Chow will learn and learn well when properly approached and when it has decided that it enjoys performing a certain command you give. Once the decision has been made to obey, there is probably no other breed which responds any more enthusiastically. I have seldom seen a Chow respond to a command with what is referred to as a "hang dog" or submissive attitude. The Chow seems to respond either with great gusto or not at all.

Never mistake your Chow's unwillingness to respond for a lack of intelligence. This is not the case at all. "Too smart for his own good" might be a better way of viewing your Chow's mental capacity. Most trainers will tell you they prefer the less intelligent breeds because they think less and are far easier to train.

This situation bears a striking parallel to what I observed while serving as an officer in the United States Army assigned to an Infantry Basic Training Battalion. I found that our field cadre preferred the less educated trainee inasmuch as orders were more apt to be obeyed without question. The training groups that came to us with a higher overall educational level were more prone to take the time to "think things out" before they responded, often asking the "reason" for a command before complying. A field soldier type your Chow is most definitely not!

After the long preceding discourse on the independent nature of the Chow—on how it alone will decide to remember something or not—I must tell you that I have never dealt with a breed as easy to housebreak as the Chow. Perhaps this is because the Chow wants to be clean, but whatever the reason, most Chowlets are housebroken in matter of days rather than weeks or months as is the case in a good number of other breeds I have worked with.

THE CRATE METHOD

First time dog owners are inclined to initially see the crate or cage method of housebreaking as cruel, but those same people will return later and thank me profusely for having suggested it in the first place. All dogs, particularly the Chow, need a place of their own to retreat to and you will find that the Chow will consider its cage that special place.

Crate training is the quickest and least stressful way to housebreak your Chow puppy.

Use of a cage reduces housetraining time down to an absolute minimum and avoids keeping a puppy under constant stress by incessantly correcting it for making mistakes in the house. The anti-cage advocates consider it cruel to confine a puppy for any length of time but find no problem in constantly harassing and punishing the puppy because it has wet on the carpet and relieved itself behind the sofa.

Chowlets can not contain themselves for very long, so take your puppy out to "go to the bathroom" often, especially after eating, drinking or vigorous playing.

Block off an area for your Chows to play in when you're not at home. Your puppies, and your belongings, will be much safer this way.

The cage used for housebreaking should only be large enough for the puppy to stand up and lie down in and to stretch out comfortably. It is not necessary to dash out and buy a new

cage every few weeks to accommodate the Chow's rapid spurts of growth. Simply cut a piece of plywood of a size to partition off the excess space in the very large cage and move it back as needed. Long before you have lost the need for the partition your Chow will be housebroken, I assure you.

Begin feeding your Chow puppy in the cage. Keep the door closed and latched while the puppy is eating. When the meal is finished, open the cage and carry the puppy outdoors to the spot where you want it to learn to eliminate. In the event you do not have outdoor access or will be away from home for long periods of time, begin housebreaking by placing newspapers in some out of the way corner that is easily accessible for the puppy. If you consistently take your puppy to the same spot you will reinforce the habit of going there for that purpose.

It is important that you do not let the puppy loose after eating. Young puppies will eliminate almost immediately after eating or drinking. They will also be ready to relieve themselves when they first wake up and after playing. If you keep a watchful eye on your Chowlet you will quickly learn when this is about to take place. A puppy usually circles and sniffs the floor just before it will relieve itself. Do not give your puppy an opportunity to learn that it can eliminate in the house! Your housetraining chores will be reduced considerably if you avoid bad habits in the first place.

If you are not able to watch your puppy every minute, it should be in its cage with the door securely latched. Each time you put your puppy in the cage, give it a small treat of some kind. Throw the treat to the back of the cage and encourage the puppy to walk in on its own. When it does so, praise the puppy and perhaps hand it another piece of the treat through the wires of the cage.

Do not succumb to your puppy's complaints about being in its cage. The puppy must learn to stay in its cage and to do so without unnecessary complaining. A quick "no" command and a tap on the crate will usually get the puppy to understand that theatrics will not result in liberation.

Do understand that a puppy of eight to twelve weeks will not be able to contain itself for long periods of time. Puppies of that age must relieve themselves every few hours except at night. Your schedule must be adjusted accordingly. Also make sure that your puppy has relieved itself both bowel and bladder the last thing at night and do not dawdle when you wake up in the morning.

Your first priority in the morning is to get the puppy outdoors. Just how early this ritual will take place will depend much more upon your puppy than upon you. If your Chowlet is like most others, there will be no doubt in your mind when it needs to be let out. You will also very quickly learn to tell the difference between the "this is an emergency" complaint and the "I just want out" grumbling. Do not test the young puppy's ability to contain itself. Its vocal demand to be let out is confirmation that the housebreaking lesson is being learned.

It is important to allow your Chow access to the outdoors first thing every morning. Mimosa is letting her owner know that its time to wake up and go out!

Should you find it necessary to be away from home all day, you will not be able to leave your puppy in a crate. On the other hand, do not make the mistake of

allowing it to roam the house or even a large room at will. Confine the puppy to a small room or partitioned area and cover the floor with newspaper. Make this area large enough so that the puppy will not have to relieve itself next to its bed or its food or water bowls. You will soon find that the puppy will be inclined to use one particular spot to perform its bowel and bladder functions. When you are home, you must take the puppy to this exact spot to eliminate at the appropriate time.

BASIC TRAINING

Where you are emotionally and the environment in which you train are just as important to your dog's training as is its state of mind at the time. Never begin training when you are irritated, distressed or preoccupied. Nor should you begin basic training in a place that interferes with you or your dog's concentration. Once the commands are understood and learned you can begin testing your dog in public places, but at first the two of you should work in a place where you can concentrate fully upon each other.

The "No" Command

There is no doubt whatsoever that one of the most important commands your Chow puppy will ever learn is the meaning of the "no" command. It is critical that the puppy learns this command just as soon as possible. One important piece of advice in using this and all other commands—never give a command you are not prepared and able to enforce! The only way a puppy learns to obey commands is to realize that once issued, commands must be obeyed. Learning the "no" command should start on the first day of the puppy's arrival at your home.

Leash Training

It is never too early to accustom the Chow puppy to a collar and leash. It is your way of keeping your dog under control. It may not be necessary for the puppy or adult Chow to wear its collar and identification tags within the confines of your home, but no Chow should ever leave home without a collar and without the leash held securely in its owner's hand.

Begin getting your Chow puppy accustomed to its collar by leaving it on for a few minutes at a time. Gradually extend the time you leave the collar on. Most Chowlets become accustomed to their collars very quickly and forget they are even wearing them.

Once this is accomplished, attach a lightweight leash to the collar while you are playing with the puppy. Do not try to guide the puppy at first. The point here is to accustom the puppy to the feeling of having something attached to the collar.

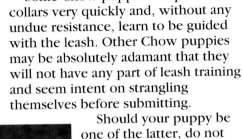

Although it might take time for him to get acclimated to it, your Chow should never leave home without his collar and tags.

Some Chow puppies adapt to their collars very quickly and, without any undue resistance, learn to be guided with the leash. Other Chow puppies may be absolutely adamant that they will not have any part of leash training and seem intent on strangling themselves before submitting.

Should your puppy be one of the latter, do not continue to force the issue. Simply create a "lasso" with your leash and put your Chowlet's head and front legs through the lasso opening so that the leash encircles the puppy's shoulders and chest, just behind the front legs. Young Chows seem to object less to this method than having the leash around their necks.

Encourage your puppy to follow you as you move away. Should the puppy be reluctant to cooperate, coax it along with a treat of some kind. Hold the treat in front of the puppy's nose to encourage it to follow you. Just as soon as the puppy takes a few steps toward you, praise it enthusiastically and keep up the praise as you continue to move along.

Make the initial session very brief and very enjoyable. Continue the lessons in your home or yard until the puppy is completely unconcerned about the fact that it is on a leash. With a treat in one hand and the leash in the other, you can begin to use both to guide the puppy in the direction you wish to go.

Once the leash around the body is taken in stride and the puppy has become accustomed to walking along with you, you can start attaching the leash to your puppy's collar. Your walks can begin in front of the house and extend down the street and eventually around the block. This is one lesson no puppy is too young to learn.

The "Come" Command

The next most important lesson for the Chow puppy to learn is to come when called; therefore, it is very important that the puppy learn its name as soon as possible. Constant repetition is what does the trick in teaching a puppy its name. Use the name every time you talk to your puppy.

Learning to "come" on command could save your Chow's life when the two of you venture out into the world. "Come" is the command that a dog must understand has to be obeyed without question, but the dog should not associate that command with fear. Your dog's response to its name and the word "come" should always be associated with a pleasant experience, such as great praise and petting or, particularly in the case of the Chow, a food treat.

It is much easier to avoid the establishment of bad habits than it is to correct them once set. Never give the "come" command unless you are sure your Chow puppy will come to you. The very young puppy is far more inclined to respond to learning the "come" command than the older Chow. Use the command initially when the puppy is already on its way to you or give the command while walking or running away from the youngster. Clap your hands and sound very happy and excited about having the puppy join in on this "game."

Teaching your Chow puppies to "come" is extremely important for their safety. If the puppies equate the command with pleasant experiences, it should easy for them to master.

The very young Chow will normally want to stay as close to its owner as possible, especially in strange surroundings. When your Chowlet sees you moving away, its natural inclination will be to get close to you. This is a perfect time to use the "come" command.

Later, as the puppy grows more independent and more headstrong as the Chow can do, you may want to attach a long leash or rope to the puppy's collar to ensure the correct response. Do not chase or punish your puppy for not obeying the "come" command. Doing so in the initial stages of training makes the youngster associate the command with something to fear and this will result in avoidance rather than the immediate positive response you desire. It is imperative that you praise your Chow puppy and give it a treat when it does come to you, even if it voluntarily delays responding for many minutes.

Whether training for the show ring or for the backyard, learning to walk on a lead is a must for any Chow.

The "Sit" and "Stay" Commands

Just as important to your Chow's safety (and your sanity!) as the "no" command and learning to come when called are the "sit" and "stay" commands. Even very young Chows can learn the sit command quickly, especially if it appears to be a game and a food treat is involved.

First, remember that the Chow-in-training should always be on collar and leash for all its lessons. A Chow is not beyond getting up and walking away when it has decided enough is enough!

Give the "sit" command immediately before pushing down on your Chow's hindquarters. Praise the dog lavishly when it does sit, even though it is you who made the action take place. Again, a food treat always seems to get the lesson across to the Chow student.

Continue holding the dog's rear end down and repeat the "sit" command several times. If your dog makes an attempt to get up, repeat the command yet again while exerting pressure on the rear end until the correct position is assumed. Make your Chow stay in this position for increasing lengths of time.

Begin with a few seconds and increase the time as lessons progress over the following weeks.

Should your Chow student attempt to get up or to lie down, it should be corrected by simply saying "sit" in a firm voice. This should be accompanied by returning the dog to the desired position. Only when *you* decide your dog should get up should it be allowed to do so. Do not push the young Chow's patience to the limit. Remember that you are dealing with a baby and the attention span of any youngster is relatively short.

When you do decide the dog can get up, call its name, say "okay" and make a big fuss over it. Praise and a food treat are in order every time your Chow responds correctly.

When teaching your Chow to "sit," hold your puppy's rear end down for a short time while repeating the command over and over— soon your pup will be sitting all by himself!

Once your Chow has mastered the "sit" lesson you may start on the "stay" command. With your Chow on leash and facing you, command it to "sit," then take a step or two back. If your dog attempts to get up to follow, firmly say "sit, stay." While you are saying this, raise your hand with your palm toward the dog and again command "stay."

Any attempt on your dog's part to get up must be corrected at once by returning it to the sit position and repeating "stay." Once your Chow begins to understand what you want, you can gradually increase the distance you step back. With a long leash (even a clothesline will do) attached to your dog's collar, start with a few steps and gradually increase the distance to several yards. Your Chow must eventually learn that the "sit, stay" command must be obeyed no matter how far away you are. Later on, with advanced training, your Chow will learn that the command is to be obeyed even when you move entirely out of sight.

As your Chow masters this lesson and is able to remain in the sit position for as long as you dictate, avoid calling the dog

Training your dog to interact and behave around people and other animals is a very important part of responsible ownership. A well-trained Chow will not jump up, even if he just wants a hug.

to you at first. This makes the dog overly anxious to get up and run to you. Instead, walk back to your dog and say "okay," which is a signal that the command is over. Later, when your Chow becomes more reliable in this respect, you can call it to you.

The "sit, stay" lesson can take considerable time and patience, especially with the Chow puppy whose attention span will be very short. It is best to keep the "stay" part of the lesson to a minimum until the Chow is five or six months old. Everything in a very young Chowlet's makeup urges it to follow you wherever you go. Forcing a very young Chow to operate against its natural instincts can be bewildering for the puppy.

The "Down" Command

Once your Chow has mastered the "sit" and "stay" commands, you may begin working on "down." This is the single word command for lie down. Use the "down" command only when you want the dog to lie down. If you want your Chow to get off your sofa or to stop jumping up on people use the "off" command. Do not interchange these two commands. Doing so will only serve to confuse your dog and evoking the right response will become next to impossible.

The "down" position is especially useful if you want your Chow to remain in a particular place for a long period of time. A Chow is far more inclined to stay put when it is lying down than when it is sitting.

Teaching this command to your Chow may take more time and patience than the previous lessons the two of you have undertaken. It is believed by some animal behaviorists that assuming the "down" position somehow represents submissiveness to the dog. Considering the highly independent nature and dominant personality of our Chows, it is easy to understand how this command could prove more difficult for them to comply with. In the end, once the "down" command has become a part of the Chow's repertory, it seems to be more relaxing for the dog. You will also find that the dog seems less inclined to get up and wander off.

With your Chow sitting in front of and facing you, hold a treat in your right hand with the excess part of the leash in your left hand. Hold the treat under the dog's nose and slowly bring your hand down to the ground. Your dog will follow the treat with its head and neck. As it does, give the command "down" and exert light pressure on the dog's shoulders with your left hand. If your dog resists the pressure on its shoulders, do not continue pushing down; doing so will only create more resistance.

An alternative method of getting your Chow headed into the down position is to move around to the dog's right side, and as you draw its attention downward with your right hand, slide your left arm under the dog's front legs and gently slide them forward. In the case of a small puppy you will undoubtedly have to be on your knees next to the youngster.

As your Chow's forelegs begin to slide out to its front, keep moving the treat along the ground until the dog's whole body is lying on the ground while you continually repeat "down." Once your Chow has assumed the position you desire, give it the treat and a lot of praise. Continue assisting your Chow into the "down" position until it does so on its own. Be firm and be patient.

The "Heel" Command

In learning to heel, your Chow will walk on your left side with its shoulder next to your leg no matter which direction you might go or how quickly you turn. Teaching your Chow to heel will not only make your daily walks far more enjoyable, it will make the dog a far more tractable companion when the two of you are in crowded or confusing situations.

Using a lightweight chain-link collar when training your dog to heel allows you to pull the dog back into position while getting his attention at the same time.

I have found that a lightweight link-chain training collar is very useful for the heeling lesson. It provides both quick pressure around the neck and a snapping sound, both of which get the

dog's attention. Erroneously referred to as a "choke collar," the link-chain collar used properly will not choke the dog. The pet shop at which you purchase the training collar will be able to show you the proper way to put this collar on your dog.

As you train your Chow puppy to walk along on the leash, you should accustom the youngster to walking on your left side. The leash should cross your body from the dog's collar to your right hand. The excess portion of the leash will be folded into your right hand, and your left hand on the leash will be used to make corrections with the leash.

A quick short jerk on the leash with your left hand will keep your Chowlet from lunging side to side, pulling ahead or lagging back. As you make a correction, give the "heel" command. Always keep the leash slack as long as your dog maintains the proper position at your side.

The Chow is an intelligent dog and once he learns any lesson, he will remember it for the rest of his life.

If your dog begins to drift away, give the leash a sharp jerk and guide the dog back to the correct position while giving the "heel" command. Do not pull on the lead with steady

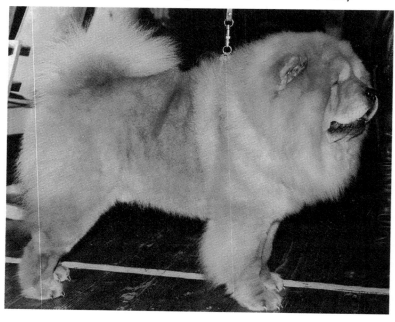

pressure. What is needed is a sharp but gentle jerking motion to get your dog's attention.

TRAINING CLASSES

There are few limits to what a patient, consistent Chow owner can teach his dog. While the Chow may not leap to perform the first time you attempt to teach it something new, take heart. Once the lesson is mastered, your Chow will perform with enthusiasm and gusto that make all the hard work well worthwhile. Don't forget, you are dealing with one of the most stubborn but also one of the most intelligent and wonderful breeds of dog known to man. Your Chow performs because it has decided it wants to, not because you are forcing it to obey. Do not tell your Chow this, but if you are persistent enough in your training your Chow will eventually think the whole thing was its own idea in the first place!

Socialization is an integral part of your Chow's training. You should be confident that your Chow will behave appropriately when taken out to new places.

For advanced obedience work beyond the basics it is wise for the Chow owner to consider local professional assistance. Professional trainers have had much experience in avoiding the pitfalls of obedience training and can help you to avoid them as well.

This training assistance can be obtained in many ways. Classes are particularly good for your Chow's socialization. There are free-of-charge classes at many parks and recreation facilities, as well as very formal and sometimes very expensive individual lessons with private trainers.

There are also some obedience schools that will take your Chow and train it for you. However, unless your schedule provides no time at all to train your own Chow, having someone else train the dog for you would be last on our list of recommendations. The rapport that develops between the owner who has trained his or her Chow to be a pleasant companion and good canine citizen is very special—well worth the time and patience it requires to achieve.

SPORT of Purebred Dogs

Welcome to the exciting and sometimes frustrating sport of dogs. No doubt you are trying to learn more about dogs or you wouldn't be deep into this book. This section covers the basics that may entice you, further your knowledge and help you to understand the dog world. If you decide to give showing, obedience or any other dog activities a try, then I suggest you seek further help from the appropriate source.

Dog showing has been a very popular sport for a long time and has been taken quite seriously by some. Others only enjoy it as a hobby.

The Kennel Club in England was formed in 1859, the American Kennel Club was established in 1884 and the Canadian Kennel Club was formed in 1888. The purpose of these clubs was to register purebred dogs and maintain their Stud Books. In the beginning, the concept of registering dogs was not readily accepted. More than 36 million dogs have been enrolled in the AKC Stud Book since its inception in 1888. Presently the kennel clubs not only register dogs but adopt and enforce rules and regulations governing dog shows, obedience trials and field trials. Over the years they have fostered and encouraged interest in the health and welfare of the purebred dog. They routinely donate funds to veterinary research for study on genetic disorders.

Below are the addresses of the kennel clubs in the United States, Great Britain and Canada.

This is Ch. Lov-Chow's Risen Star, a multiple Best of Breed and Best in Show winner, with his co-owner and handler, Michael Larissa.

The American Kennel Club
51 Madison Avenue
New York, NY 10010
(Their registry is located at: 5580 Centerview Drive, STE 200, Raleigh, NC 27606-3390)

The Kennel Club
1 Clarges Street
Piccadilly, London, WIY 8AB, England

The Canadian Kennel Club
111 Eglinton Avenue
East Toronto, Ontario M6S 4V7
Canada

Today there are numerous activities that are enjoyable for both the dog and the handler. Some of the activities include conformation showing, obedience competition, tracking, agility, the Canine Good Citizen Certificate, and a wide range of instinct tests that vary from breed to breed. Where you start depends upon your goals which early on may not be readily apparent.

PUPPY KINDERGARTEN

Every puppy will benefit from this class. PKT is the foundation for all future dog activities from conformation to "couch potatoes." Pet owners should make an effort to attend even if they never expect to show their dog. The class is designed for puppies about three months of age with graduation at approximately five months of age. All the puppies will be in the same age group and, even though some may be a little unruly, there should not be any real problem. This class will teach the puppy some beginning obedience. As in all obedience classes the owner learns how to train his own dog. The PKT class gives the puppy the opportunity to interact with other puppies in the same age group and exposes him to

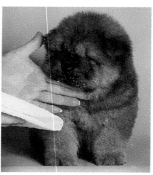

strangers, which is very important. Some dogs grow up with behavior problems, one of them being fear of strangers. As you can see, there can be much to gain from this class.

Prior to six months of age you may show in puppy matches to allow your Chow to become acquainted with the ring procedures.

Why is this dog wearing a bib? Because it's "Chow" time!

CONFORMATION

Conformation showing is our oldest dog show sport. This type of showing is based on the dog's appearance—that is his structure, movement and attitude. When considering this type of showing, you need to be aware of your breed's standard and be able to evaluate your dog compared to that standard. The breeder of your puppy or other experienced breeders would be good sources for such an evaluation. Puppies can go through lots of changes over a period of time. I always say most puppies start out as promising hopefuls and then after maturing may be disappointing as show candidates. Even so this should not deter them from being excellent pets.

Usually conformation training classes are offered by the local kennel or obedience clubs. These are excellent places for training puppies. The puppy should be able to walk on a lead before entering such a class. Proper ring procedure and technique for posing (stacking) the dog will be demonstrated as well as gaiting the dog. Usually certain patterns are used in the ring such as the triangle or the "L." Conformation class, like the PKT class, will give your youngster the opportunity to socialize with different breeds of dogs and humans too.

It takes some time to learn the routine of conformation showing. Usually one starts at the puppy matches which may be AKC Sanctioned or Fun Matches. These matches are generally for puppies from two or three months to a year old, and there may be classes for the adult over the age of 12 months. Similar to point shows, the classes are divided by sex and after completion of the classes in that breed or variety, the class winners compete for Best of Breed or Variety. The winner goes on to compete in the Group and the Group winners compete for Best in Match. No championship points are awarded for match wins.

A few matches can be great training for puppies even though there is no intention to go on showing. Matches enable the puppy to meet new people and be handled by a stranger— the judge. It is also a change of environment, which broadens the horizon for both dog and handler. Matches and other dog activities boost the confidence of the handler and especially the younger handlers.

Earning an AKC championship is built on a point system, which is different from Great Britain. To become an AKC Champion of Record the dog must earn 15 points. The number of points earned each time depends upon the number of dogs in competition. The number of points available at each show depends upon the breed, its sex and the location of the show. The United States is divided into ten AKC zones. Each zone has its own set of points. The purpose of the zones is to try to equalize the points available from breed to breed and area to area.The AKC adjusts the point scale annually.

The number of points that can be won at a show are between one and five. Three- four- and five-point wins are considered majors. Not only does the dog need 15 points won under three different judges, but those points must include two majors under two different judges. Canada also works on a point system but majors are not required.

Dogs always show before bitches. The classes available to those seeking points are: Puppy (which may be divided into 6 to 9 months and 9 to 12 months); 12 to 18 months; Novice; Bred-by-Exhibitor; American-bred; and Open. The class winners of the same sex of each breed or variety compete against each other for Winners Dog and Winners Bitch. A Reserve Winners Dog and Reserve Winners Bitch are also awarded but do not carry any points unless the Winners win is disallowed by AKC. The Winners Dog and Bitch compete with the specials (those dogs that have attained championship) for Best of Breed or Variety, Best of Winners and Best of Opposite Sex. It is possible to pick up an extra point or even a major if the points are higher for the defeated winner than those of Best of Winners. The latter would get the higher total from the defeated winner.

At an all-breed show, each Best of Breed or Variety winner will go on to his respective Group and then the Group winners will compete against each other for Best in Show. There are seven Groups: Sporting, Hounds, Working, Terriers, Toys, Non-Sporting and Herding. Obviously there are no Groups at speciality shows (those

This is the 1995 Supreme Chow and Best in Show winner Ch. My-Sam's Knight in New York with Bob Boughart.

shows that have only one breed or a show such as the American Spaniel Club's Flushing Spaniel Show, which is for all flushing spaniel breeds).

Earning a championship in England is somewhat different since they do not have a point system. Challenge Certificates are awarded if the judge feels the dog is deserving regardless of the number of dogs in competition. A dog must earn three Challenge Certificates under three different judges, with at least one of these Certificates being won after the age of 12 months. Competition is very strong and entries may be higher than they are in the U.S. The Kennel Club's Challenge Certificates are only available at Championship Shows.

In England, The Kennel Club regulations require that certain dogs, Border Collies and Gundog breeds, qualify in a working capacity (i.e., obedience or field trials) before becoming a full Champion. If they do not qualify in the working aspect, then they are designated a Show Champion, which is equivalent to the AKC's Champion of Record. A Gundog may be granted the title of Field Trial Champion (FT Ch.) if it passes all the tests in the field but would also have to qualify in conformation before becoming a full Champion. A Border Collie that earns the title of Obedience Champion (Ob Ch.) must also qualify in the conformation ring before becoming a Champion.

The U.S. doesn't have a designation full Champion but does award for Dual and Triple Champions. The Dual Champion must be a Champion of Record, and either Champion Tracker, Herding Champion, Obedience Trial Champion or Field Champion. Any dog that has been awarded the titles of

Chow Chow dogs that compete in conformation must be perfectly groomed for presentation in the show ring.

Champion of Record, and any two of the following: Champion Tracker, Herding Champion, Obedience Trial Champion or Field Champion, may be designated as a Triple Champion.

The shows in England seem to put more emphasis on breeder judges than those in the U.S. There is much competition within the breeds. Therefore the quality of the individual breeds should be very good. In the United States we tend to have more "all around judges" (those that judge multiple breeds) and use the breeder judges at the specialty shows. Breeder judges are more familiar with their own breed since they are actively breeding that breed or did so at one time. Americans emphasize Group and Best in Show wins and promote them accordingly.

Celestial's Beach Buccaneer waits patiently in his crate for his turn in the spotlight.

It is my understanding that the shows in England can be very large and extend over several days, with the Groups being scheduled on different days. I believe there is only one all-breed show in the U.S. that extends over two days, the Westminster Kennel Club Show. In our country we have cluster shows, where several different clubs will use the same show site over consecutive days.

Westminster Kennel Club is our most prestigious show although the entry is limited to 2500. In recent years, entry has been limited to Champions. This show is more formal than the majority of the shows with the judges wearing formal attire and the handlers fashionably dressed. In most instances the quality of the dogs is superb. After all, it is a show of Champions. It is a good show to study the AKC registered breeds and is by far the most exciting—especially since it is televised! WKC is one of the few shows in this country that is still benched. This means the dog must be in his benched area during the show hours except when he is being groomed, in the ring, or being exercised.

Typically, the handlers are very particular about their appearances. They are careful not to wear something that will detract from their dog but will perhaps enhance it. American ring procedure is quite formal compared to that of other countries. I remember being reprimanded by a judge because I made a suggestion to a friend holding my second dog outside the ring. I certainly could have used more discretion so I would not call attention to myself. There is a certain etiquette expected between the judge and exhibitor and among the other exhibitors. Of course it is not always the case but the judge is supposed to be polite, not engaging in small talk or even acknowledging that he knows the handler. I understand that there is a more informal and relaxed atmosphere at the shows in other countries. For instance, the dress code is more casual. I can see where this might be more fun for the exhibitor and especially for the novice. This country is very handler-oriented in many of the breeds. It is true, in most instances, that the experienced professional handler can present the dog better and will have a feel for what a judge likes.

Handlers should wear comfortable clothing that does not restrict their movement or distract from the dog.

In England, Crufts is The Kennel Club's own show and is most assuredly the largest dog show in the world. They've been known to have an entry of nearly 20,000, and the show lasts four days. Entry is only gained by qualifying through winning in specified classes at another Championship Show. Westminster is strictly conformation, but Crufts exhibitors and spectators enjoy not only conformation but obedience, agility and a multitude of exhibitions as well. Obedience was admitted in 1957 and agility in 1983.

If you are handling your own dog, please give some consideration to your apparel. For sure the dress code at matches is more informal than the point shows. However, you should wear something a little more appropriate than beach attire or ragged jeans and bare feet. If you check out the handlers and see what is presently fashionable, you'll catch on. Men usually dress with a shirt and tie and a nice sports coat. Whether you are male or female, you will want to wear comfortable clothes and shoes. You need to be able to run with your dog and you certainly don't want to take a chance of falling and hurting yourself.

There are many accessories that you need to bring when going to a show, including your crate, ex pen, grooming equipment, and clean up materials.

Heaven forbid, if nothing else, you'll upset your dog. Women usually wear a dress or two-piece outfit, preferably with pockets to carry bait, comb, brush, etc. In this case men are the lucky ones with all their pockets. Ladies, think about where your dress will be if you need to kneel on the floor and also think about running. Does it allow freedom to do so?

Years ago, after toting around all the baby paraphernalia, I found toting the dog and necessities a breeze. You need to take along dog; crate; ex pen (if you use one); extra newspaper; water pail and water; all required grooming equipment, including hair dryer and extension cord; table; chair for you; bait for dog and lunch for you and friends; and, last but not least, clean up materials, such as plastic bags, paper towels, and perhaps a bath towel and some shampoo—just in case. Don't forget your entry confirmation and directions to the show.

If you are showing in obedience, then you will want to wear pants. Many of our top obedience handlers wear pants that are color-coordinated with their dogs. The philosophy is that imperfections in the black dog will be less obvious next to your black pants.

Whether you are showing in conformation, Junior Showmanship or obedience, you need to watch the clock and be sure you are not late. It is customary to pick up your conformation armband a few minutes before the start of the class. They will not wait for you and if you are on the show grounds and not in the ring, you will upset everyone. It's a little more complicated picking up your obedience armband if you show later in the class. If you have not picked up your armband and they get to your number, you may not be allowed to show. It's best to pick up your armband early, but then you may show earlier than expected if other handlers don't pick up. Customarily all conflicts should be discussed with the judge prior to the start of the class.

CANINE GOOD CITIZEN

The AKC sponsors a program to encourage dog owners to train their dogs. Local clubs perform the pass/fail tests, and dogs who pass are awarded a Canine Good Citizen Certificate. Proof of vaccination is required at the time of participation. The test includes:

1. Accepting a friendly stranger.
2. Sitting politely for petting.
3. Appearance and grooming.
4. Walking on a loose leash.
5. Walking through a crowd.
6. Sit and down on command/staying in place.
7. Come when called.
8. Reaction to another dog.
9. Reactions to distractions.
10. Supervised separation.

If more effort was made by pet owners to accomplish these exercises, fewer dogs would be cast off to the humane shelter.

OBEDIENCE

Obedience is necessary, without a doubt, but it can also become a wonderful hobby or even an obsession. In my opinion, obedience classes and competition can provide wonderful companionship, not only with your dog but with your classmates or fellow competitors. It is always gratifying to discuss your dog's problems with others who have had similar experiences. The AKC acknowledged Obedience around 1936, and it has changed tremendously even though many of the exercises are basically the same. Today, obedience competition is just that—very competitive. Even so, it is possible for every obedience exhibitor to come home a winner (by earning qualifying scores) even though he/she may not earn a placement in the class.

Even if you do not show your Chow, he can win the Canine Good Citizen certificate by demonstrating that he is an even-tempered and well-trained pet.

Most of the obedience titles are awarded after earning three qualifying scores (legs) in the appropriate class under three different judges. These classes offer a perfect score of 200, which is extremely rare. Each of the class exercises has its own point value. A leg is earned after receiving a score of at least 170 and at least 50 percent of the points available in each exercise.

TRACKING

Tracking is officially classified obedience, but I feel it should have its own category. There are three tracking titles available: Tracking Dog (TD), Tracking Dog Excellent (TDX), Variable Surface Tracking (VST). If all three tracking titles are obtained, then the dog officially becomes a CT (Champion Tracker). The CT will go in front of the dog's name.

A TD may be earned anytime and does not have to follow the other obedience titles. There are many exhibitors that prefer tracking to obedience, and there are others like myself that do both. In my experience with small dogs, I prefer to earn the CD and CDX before attempting tracking. My reasoning is that small dogs are closer to the mat in the obedience rings and therefore it's too easy to put the nose down and sniff. Tracking encourages sniffing. Of course this depends on the dog. I've had some dogs that tracked around the ring and others (TDXs) who wouldn't think of sniffing in the ring.

AGILITY

Agility was first introduced by John Varley in England at the Crufts Dog Show, February 1978, but Peter Meanwell, competitor and judge, actually developed the idea. It was officially recognized in the early '80s. Agility is extremely popular in England and Canada and growing in popularity in the U.S. The AKC acknowledged agility in August 1994. Dogs must be at least 12 months of age to be entered. It is a fascinating sport that the dog, handler and spectators enjoy to the utmost. Agility is a spectator sport! The dog performs off lead. The handler either runs with his dog or positions himself on the course and directs his dog with verbal and hand signals over a timed course over or through a variety of obstacles including a time out or pause. One of the main drawbacks to agility is finding a place to train. The obstacles take up a lot of space and it is very time consuming to put up and take down courses.

The titles earned at AKC agility trials are Novice Agility Dog (NAD), Open Agility Dog (OAD), Agility Dog Excellent (ADX), and Master Agility Excellent (MAX). In order to acquire an agility title, a dog must earn a qualifying score in its respective class on three separate occasions under two different judges. The MAX will be awarded after earning ten qualifying scores in the Agility Excellent Class.

GENERAL INFORMATION

Obedience, tracking and agility allow the purebred dog with an Indefinite Listing Privilege (ILP) number or a limited registration to be exhibited and earn titles. Application must be made to the AKC for an ILP number.

The American Kennel Club publishes a monthly *Events* magazine that is part of the *Gazette*, their official journal for the sport of purebred dogs. The *Events* section lists upcoming shows and the secretary or superintendent for them. The majority of the conformation shows in the U.S. are overseen by licensed superintendents. Generally the entry closing date is approximately two-and-a-half weeks before the actual show. Point shows are fairly expensive, while the match shows cost about one third of the point show entry fee. Match shows usually take entries the day of the show but some are pre-entry. The best way to find match show information is through your local kennel club. Upon asking, the AKC can provide you with a list of superintendents, and you can write and ask to be put on their mailing lists.

Obedience trial and tracking test information is available through the AKC. Frequently these events are not superintended, but put on by the host club. Therefore you would make the entry with the event's secretary.

As you have read, there are numerous activities you can share with your dog. Regardless what you do, it does take teamwork. Your dog can only benefit from your attention and training. I hope this chapter has enlightened you and hope, if nothing else, you will attend a show here and there. Perhaps you will start with a puppy kindergarten class, and who knows where it may lead!

Although her full name is Ch. Rebelrun Knight Time, all her friends know this beautiful red chow as "Peaches."

BEHAVIOR and Canine Communication

Studies of the human/animal bond point out the importance of the unique relationships that exist between people and their pets. Those of us who share our lives with pets understand the special part they play through companionship, service and protection. For many, the pet/owner bond goes beyond simple companionship; pets are often considered members of the family.

Senior citizens show more concern for their own eating habits when they have the responsibility of feeding a dog. Seeing that their dog is routinely exercised encourages the owner to think of schedules that otherwise may seem unimportant to the senior citizen. The older owner may be arthritic and feeling poorly but with responsibility for his dog he has a reason to get up and get moving. It is a big plus if his dog is an attention seeker who will demand such from his owner.

The majority of Chows live in family environments, and have to conform to the rules of the household.

Over the last couple of decades, it has been shown that pets relieve the stress of those who lead busy lives. Owning a pet has been known to lessen the occurrence of heart attack and stroke.

Many single folks thrive on the companionship of a dog. Lifestyles are very different from a long time ago, and today more individuals seek the single life. However, they receive fulfillment from owning a dog.

Most likely the majority of our dogs live in family environments. The companionship they provide is well worth the effort involved. In my opinion, every child should have the opportunity to have a family dog. Dogs teach responsibility

Taking responsibility for a dog can give a person a purpose in life. Of course, playing with an adorable Chow puppy can brighten anybody's day.

through understanding their care, feelings and even respecting their life cycles. Frequently those children who have not been exposed to dogs grow up afraid of dogs, which isn't good. Dogs sense timidity and some will take advantage of the situation.

Today more dogs are serving as service dogs. Since the origination of the Seeing Eye dogs years ago, we now have trained hearing dogs. Also dogs are trained to provide service for the handicapped and are able to perform many different tasks for their owners. Search and Rescue dogs, with their handlers, are sent throughout the world to assist in recovery of disaster victims. They are life savers.

The Chow is a breed that thrives on social interaction. Although they may act aloof at times, they love to get their owners' attention.

Therapy dogs are very popular with nursing homes, and some hospitals even allow them to visit. The inhabitants truly look forward to their visits. I have taken a couple of my dogs visiting and left in tears when I saw the response of the patients. They wanted and were allowed to have my dogs in their beds to hold and love.

Nationally there is a Pet Awareness Week to educate students and others about the value and basic care of our pets. Many countries take an even greater interest in their pets than Americans do. In those countries the pets are allowed to accompany their owners into restaurants and shops, etc. In the U.S. this freedom is only available to our service dogs. Even so we think very highly of the human/animal bond.

CANINE BEHAVIOR

Canine behavior problems are the number-one reason for pet owners to dispose of their dogs, either through new homes, humane shelters or euthanasia. Unfortunately there are too many owners who are unwilling to devote the necessary time to properly train their dogs. On the other hand, there are those who not only are concerned about inherited health problems but are also aware of the dog's mental stability. You may realize that a breed and his group relatives (i.e., sporting, hounds, etc.) show tendencies to behavioral characteristics. An experienced breeder can acquaint you with his breed's personality. Unfortunately many breeds are labeled with poor temperaments when actually the breed as a whole is not affected but only a small percentage of individuals within the breed.

Temperament is a combination of breeding and environment. Unfortunately many breeds are labeled "bad tempered" because their owners do not properly train them.

If the breed in question is very popular, then of course there may be a higher number of unstable dogs. Do not label a breed good or bad. I know of absolutely awful-tempered dogs within one of our most popular, lovable breeds.

Inheritance and environment contribute to the dog's behavior. Some naïve people suggest inbreeding as the cause of bad temperaments. Inbreeding only results in poor behavior if the ancestors carry the trait. If there are excellent temperaments behind the dogs, then inbreeding will promote good temperaments in the offspring. Did you ever consider that inbreeding is what sets the characteristics of a breed? A purebred dog is the end result of inbreeding. This does not spare the mixed-breed dog from the same problems. Mixed-breed dogs frequently are the offspring of purebred dogs.

When planning a breeding, I like to observe the potential stud and his offspring in the show ring. If I see unruly behavior, I try to look into it further. I want to know if it is genetic or environmental, due to the lack of training and socialization. A good breeder will avoid breeding mentally unsound dogs.

Not too many decades ago most of our dogs led a different lifestyle than what is prevalent today. Usually mom stayed home so the dog had human companionship and someone to discipline it if needed. Not much was expected from the dog. Today's mom works and everyone's life is at a much faster pace.

The dog may have to adjust to being a "weekend" dog. The family is gone all day during the week, and the dog is left to his own devices for entertainment. Some dogs sleep all day waiting for their family to come home and others become wigwam wreckers if given the opportunity. Crates do ensure the safety of the dog and the house. However, he could become a physically and emotionally cripple if he doesn't get enough exercise and attention. We still appreciate and want the companionship of our dogs although we expect more from them. In many cases we tend to forget dogs are just that—*dogs* not human beings.

I own several dogs who are left crated during the day but I do try to make time for them in the evenings and on the weekends. Also we try to do something together before I leave for work. Maybe it helps them to have the companionship of other dogs. They accept their crates as their personal "houses" and seem to be content with their routine and thrive on trying their best to please me.

Socializing and Training

Many prospective puppy buyers lack experience regarding the proper socialization and training needed to develop the type of pet we all desire. In the first 18 months, training does take some work. Trust me, it is easier to start proper training before there is a problem that needs to be corrected.

Socialization is very important for all dogs. This Chow has taken it upon himself to make his own friends!

Because of today's busy lifestyles, some dogs have to adjust to receiving less attention from their families. Always remember to make time for your Chow.

The initial work begins with the breeder. The breeder should start socializing the puppy at five to six weeks of age and cannot let up. Human socializing is critical up through 12 weeks of age and likewise important during the following months. The litter should be left together during the first few weeks but it is necessary to separate them by ten weeks of age. Leaving them together after that time will increase competition for litter dominance. If puppies are not socialized with people by 12 weeks of age, they will be timid in later life.

The eight- to ten-week age period is a fearful time for puppies. They need to be handled very gently around children and adults. There should be no harsh discipline during this time. Starting at 14 weeks of age, the puppy begins the juvenile period, which ends when he reaches sexual maturity around six to 14 months of age. During the juvenile period he needs to be introduced to strangers (adults, children and other dogs) on the home property. At sexual maturity he will begin to bark at strangers and become more protective. Males start to lift their legs to urinate but if you desire you can inhibit this behavior by walking your boy on leash away from trees, shrubs, fences, etc.

Perhaps you are thinking about an older puppy. You need to inquire about the puppy's social experience. If he has lived in a kennel, he may have a hard time adjusting to people and environmental stimuli. Assuming he has had a good social upbringing, there are advantages to an older puppy.

Training includes puppy kindergarten and a minimum of one to two basic training classes. During these classes you will learn how to dominate your youngster. This is especially important if you own a large breed of dog. It is somewhat harder, if not nearly impossible, for some owners to be the Alpha figure when their dog towers over them. You will be taught how to properly restrain your dog. This concept is important. Again it puts you in the Alpha position. All dogs need to be restrained many times during their lives. Believe it or not, some of our worst offenders are the eight-week-old puppies that are brought to our clinic. They need to be gently restrained for a nail trim but the way they carry on you would think we were killing them. In comparison, their vaccination is a "piece of cake." When we ask dogs to do something that is not agreeable to them, then their worst comes out. Life will be easier for your dog if you expose him at a young age to the necessities of life—proper behavior and restraint.

Understanding the Dog's Language

Most authorities agree that the dog is a descendent of the wolf. The dog and wolf have similar traits. For instance both are pack oriented and prefer not to be isolated for long periods of time. Another characteristic is that the dog, like the wolf, looks to the leader—Alpha—for direction. Both the wolf and the dog communicate through body language, not only within their pack but with outsiders.

Every pack has an Alpha figure. The dog looks to you, or should look to you, to be that leader. If your dog doesn't receive the proper training and guidance, he very well may replace you as Alpha. This would be a serious problem and is certainly a disservice to your dog.

Eye contact is one way the Alpha wolf keeps order within his pack. You are Alpha so you must establish eye contact with your puppy. Obviously your puppy will have to look at you. Practice eye contact even if you need to hold his head for five to ten seconds at a time. You can give him a treat as a reward.

Make sure your eye contact is gentle and not threatening. Later, if he has been naughty, it is permissible to give him a long, penetrating look. I caution you there are some older dogs that never learned eye contact as puppies and cannot accept eye contact. You should avoid eye contact with these dogs since they feel threatened and will retaliate as such.

Body Language

The play bow, when the forequarters are down and the hindquarters are elevated, is an invitation to play. Puppies play fight, which helps them learn the acceptable limits of biting. This is necessary for later in their lives.

You can tell by this Chow's body language that he retains many qualities of his guard dog ancestors.

Nevertheless, an owner may be falsely reassured by the playful nature of his dog's aggression. Playful aggression toward another dog or human may be an indication of serious aggression in the future. Owners should never play fight or play tug-of-war with any dog that is inclined to be dominant.

Signs of submission are:

1. Avoids eye contact.
2. Active submission—the dog crouches down, ears back and the tail is lowered.
3. Passive submission—the dog rolls on his side with his hindlegs in the air and frequently urinates.

Signs of dominance are:

1. Makes eye contact.
2. Stands with ears up, tail up and the hair raised on his neck.
3. Shows dominance over another dog by standing at right angles over it.

Dominant dogs tend to behave in characteristic ways such as:

1. The dog may be unwilling to move from his place (i.e.,

reluctant to give up the sofa if the owner wants to sit there).

2. He may not part with toys or objects in his mouth and may show possessiveness with his food bowl.

3. He may not respond quickly to commands.

4. He may be disagreeable for grooming and dislikes to be petted.

Dogs are popular because of their sociable nature. Those that have contact with humans during the first 12 weeks of life regard them as a member of their own species—their pack. All dogs have the potential for both dominant and submissive behavior. Only through experience and training do they learn to whom it is appropriate to show which behavior. Not all dogs are concerned with dominance but owners need to be aware of that potential. It is wise for the owner to establish his dominance early on.

Dogs that have contact with humans very early in life regard people as members of their "pack" - in fact, even as members of their species.

A human can express dominance or submission toward a dog in the following ways:

1. Meeting the dog's gaze signals dominance. Averting the gaze signals submission. If the dog growls or threatens, averting the gaze is the first avoiding action to take—it may prevent attack. It is important to establish eye contact in the puppy. The older dog that has not been exposed to eye contact may see it as a threat and will not be willing to submit.

Guarding his food bowl is a sign of dominance in a puppy. You must teach your Chow who is boss from the very beginning of your relationship.

2. Being taller than the dog signals dominance; being lower signals submission. This is why, when attempting to make friends with a strange dog or catch the runaway, one should kneel down to his level. Some owners see their dogs become dominant when allowed on the furniture or on the bed. Then he is at the owner's level.

3. An owner can gain dominance by ignoring all the dog's social initiatives. The owner pays attention to the dog only when he obeys a command.

No dog should be allowed to achieve dominant status over any adult or child. Ways of preventing are as follows:

1. Handle the puppy gently, especially during the three- to four-month period.

2. Let the children and adults handfeed him and teach him to take food without lunging or grabbing.

3. Do not allow him to chase children or joggers.

4. Do not allow him to jump on people or mount their legs. Even females may be inclined to mount. It is not only a male habit.

5. Do not allow him to growl for any reason.

6. Don't participate in wrestling or tug-of-war games.

7. Don't physically punish puppies for aggressive behavior. Restrain him from repeating the infraction and teach an alternative behavior. Dogs should earn everything

they receive from their owners. This would include sitting to receive petting or treats, sitting before going out the door and sitting to receive the collar and leash. These types of exercises reinforce the owner's dominance.

Young children should never be left alone with a dog. It is important that children learn some basic obedience commands so they have some control over the dog. They will gain the respect of their dog.

FEAR

One of the most common problems dogs experience is being fearful. Some dogs are more afraid than others. On the lesser side, which is sometimes humorous to watch, my dog can be afraid of a strange object. He acts silly when something is out of place in the house. I call his problem perceptive intelligence. He realizes the abnormal within his known environment. He does not react the same way in strange environments since he does not know what is normal.

If your Chow is overly fearful, you may be able to coax him towards you with a treat. This Chow can't resist his favorite Gumabone®.

On the more serious side is a fear of people. This can result in

Sitze-Gou's Rau'n Glazz, owned by Paulette Braun and Charlene Niles, is a perfect example of the Chow Chow's dignified, independent demeanor.

backing off, seeking his own space and saying "leave me alone" or it can result in an aggressive behavior that may lead to challenging the person. Respect that the dog wants to be left alone and give him time to come forward. If you approach the cornered dog, he may resort to snapping. If you leave him alone, he may decide to come forward, which should be rewarded with a treat. Years ago we had a dog that behaved in this manner. We coaxed people to stop by the house and make friends with our fearful dog. She learned to take the treats and after weeks of work she overcame her suspicions and made friends more readily.

Some dogs may initially be too fearful to take treats. In these cases it is helpful to make sure the dog hasn't eaten for about 24 hours. Being a little hungry encourages him to accept the treats, especially if they are of the "gourmet" variety. I have a dog that worries about strangers since people seldom stop by my house. Over the years she has learned a cue and jumps up quickly to visit anyone sitting on the sofa. She learned by herself that all guests on the sofa were to be trusted friends. I think she felt more comfortable with them being at her level, rather than towering over her.

Dogs can be afraid of numerous things, including loud noises and thunderstorms. Invariably the owner rewards (by comforting) the dog when it shows signs of fearfulness. I had a terrible problem with my favorite dog in the Utility obedience class. Not only was he intimidated in the class but he was afraid of noise and afraid of displeasing me. Frequently he would knock down the bar jump, which clattered dreadfully. I gave him credit because he continued to try to clear it, although he was terribly scared. I finally learned to "reward" him every time he knocked down the jump. I would jump up and down, clap my hands and tell him how great he was. My psychology worked, he relaxed and eventually cleared the jump with ease. When your dog is frightened, direct his attention to something else and act happy. Don't dwell on his fright.

AGGRESSION

Some different types of aggression are: predatory, defensive, dominance, possessive, protective, fear induced, noise provoked, "rage" syndrome (unprovoked aggression), maternal and aggression directed toward other dogs. Aggression is the most common behavioral problem encountered. Protective breeds are expected to be more aggressive than others but with the proper upbringing they can make very dependable companions. You need to be able to read your dog.

Many factors contribute to aggression including genetics and environment. An improper environment, which may include the living conditions, lack of social life, excessive punishment, being attacked or frightened by an aggressive dog, etc., can all influence a dog's behavior. Even spoiling him and giving too much praise may be detrimental. Isolation and the lack of human contact or exposure to frequent teasing by children or adults also can ruin a good dog.

Lack of direction, fear, or confusion lead to aggression in those dogs that are so inclined. Any obedience exercise, even the sit and down, can direct the dog and overcome fear and/or confusion. Every dog should learn these commands as a youngster, and there should be periodic reinforcement.

When a dog is showing signs of aggression, you should speak calmly (no screaming or hysterics) and firmly give a command that he understands, such as the sit. As soon as your dog obeys, you have assumed your dominant position. Aggression presents a problem because there may be danger to others. Sometimes it is an emotional issue. Owners may consciously or unconsciously encourage their dog's aggression. Other owners show responsibility by accepting the problem and taking measures to keep it under control. The owner is responsible for his dog's actions, and it is not wise to take a chance on someone being bitten, especially a child. Euthanasia is the solution for some owners and in severe cases this may be the best choice. However, few dogs are that dangerous and very few are that much of a threat to their owners. If caution is exercised and professional help is gained early on, then I surmise most cases can be controlled.

If your Chow understands obedience commands such as "stay" and "down" he will assuredly be considered a well-mannered pet and will be welcomed in any home.

Some authorities recommend feeding a lower protein (less than 20 percent) diet. They believe this can aid in reducing aggression. If the dog loses weight, then vegetable oil can be added. Veterinarians and behaviorists are having some success with pharmacology. In many cases treatment is possible and can improve the situation.

If you have done everything according to "the book" regarding training and socializing and are still having a behavior problem, don't procrastinate. It is important that the problem gets attention before it is out of hand. It is estimated that 20 percent of a veterinarian's time may be devoted to dealing with problems before they become so intolerable that the dog is separated from its home and owner. If your veterinarian isn't able to help, he should refer you to a behaviorist.

PROBLEMS

Barking

This is a habit that shouldn't be encouraged. Over the years I've had new puppy owners call to say that their dog hasn't learned to bark. I assure them they are indeed fortunate but not to worry. Some owners desire their dog to bark so as to be a watchdog. In my experience, most dogs will bark when a stranger comes to the door.

The new puppy frequently barks or whines in the crate in his strange environment and the owner reinforces the puppy's bad behavior by going to him during the night. This is a no-no. I tell my new owners to smack the top of the crate and say "quiet" in a loud, firm voice. The puppies don't like to hear the loud noise of the crate being banged. If the barking is sleep-interrupting, then the owner should take crate and pup to the bedroom for a few days until the puppy becomes adjusted to his new environment. Otherwise ignore the barking during the night.

Ch. Rebelrun's Peppermint Twist, otherwise known as Twister, is six months old and ready to take on the world — if someone would only help him down.

Barking can be an inherited problem or a bad habit learned through the environment. It takes dedication to stop the barking. Attention should be paid to the cause of the barking. Does the dog seek attention, does he need to go out, is it feeding time, is it occurring when he is left alone, is it a protective bark, etc.? Presently I have a ten-week-old puppy that is a real loud mouth, which I am sure is an inherited tendency. Both her mother and especially her grandmother are overzealous barkers but fortunately have mellowed with the years. My young puppy is corrected with a firm "no" and gentle shaking and she is responding. When barking presents a problem for you, try to stop it as soon as it begins.

Dogs often jump up as a sign of affection. Some people love to be greeted in this manner, but others do not appreciate paw prints on their good clothes!

There are electronic collars available that are supposed to curb barking. Personally I have not had experience with them. There are some disadvantages to to the collar. If the dog is barking out of excitement, punishment is not the appropriate treatment. Presumably there is the chance the collar could be activated by other stimuli and thereby punish the dog when it is not barking. Should you decide to use one, then you should seek help from a person with experience with that type of collar. In my opinion I feel the root of the problem needs to be investigated and corrected.

In extreme circumstances (usually when there is a problem with the neighbors), some people have resorted to having their dogs debarked. I caution you that the dog continues to bark but usually only a squeaking sound is heard. Frequently the vocal cords grow back. Probably the biggest concern is that the dog can be left with scar tissue which can narrow the opening to the trachea.

Jumping Up

Personally, I am not thrilled when other dogs jump on me but I have hurt feelings if they don't! I do encourage my own dogs to jump on me, on command. Some do and some don't. In my opinion, a dog that jumps up is a happy dog. Nevertheless few guests appreciate dogs jumping on them. Clothes get footprinted and/or snagged.

I am a believer in allowing the puppy to jump up during his first few weeks. In my opinion if you correct him too soon and at the wrong age you may intimidate him. Consequently he could be timid around humans later in his life. However, there will come a time, probably around four months of age, that he needs to know when it is okay to jump and when he is to show off good manners by sitting instead.

Some authorities never allow jumping. If you are irritated by your dog jumping up on you, then you should discourage it from the beginning. A larger breed of dog can cause harm to a senior citizen. Some are quite fragile. It may not take much to cause a topple that could break a hip.

How do you correct the problem? All family members need to participate in teaching the puppy to sit as soon as he starts to jump up. The sit must be practiced every time he starts to jump up. Don't forget to praise him for his good behavior. If an older dog has acquired the habit, grasp his paws and squeeze tightly. Give a firm "No." He'll soon catch on. Remember the entire family must take part. Each time you allow him to jump up you go back a step in training.

Biting

All puppies bite and try to chew on your fingers, toes, arms, etc. This is the time to teach them to be gentle and not bite hard. Put your fingers in your puppy's mouth and if he bites too hard then say "easy" and let him know he's hurting you. I squeal and act like I have been seriously hurt. If the puppy plays too rough and doesn't respond to your corrections, then he needs "Time Out" in his crate. You should be particularly careful with young children and puppies who still have their deciduous (baby) teeth. Those teeth are like needles and can leave little scars on youngsters. My adult daughter still has a small scar on her face from when she teased an eight-week-old puppy as an eight-year-old.

Biting in the more mature dog is something that should be prevented at all costs. Should it occur I would quickly let him know in no uncertain terms that biting will not be tolerated. When biting is directed toward another dog (dog fight), don't get in the middle of it. On more than one occasion I have had to separate a couple of my dogs and usually was in the middle of that one last lunge by the offender. Some authorities recommend breaking up a fight by elevating the hind legs. This would only be possible if there was a person for each dog. Obviously it would be hard to fight with the hind legs off the ground. A dog bite is serious and should be given attention. Wash the bite with soap and water and contact your doctor. It is important to know the status of the offender's rabies vaccination.

All puppies will chew on anything, even your fingers. Teach him to be gentle with people and give him a Nylabone® to play with instead.

I have several dogs that are sensitive to having mats combed out of their coats and eventually they have had enough. They give fair warning by turning and acting like they would like to nip my offending fingers. However, one verbal warning from me says, "I'm sorry, don't you dare think about biting me and please let me carefully comb just a little bit more." I have owned a minimum of 30 dogs and raised many more puppies and have yet to have one of my dogs bite me except during that last lunge in the two or three dog fights I felt compelled to break up. My dogs wouldn't dare bite me. They know who is boss.

This is not always the case for other owners. I do not wish to frighten you but when biting occurs you should seek professional help at once. On the other hand you must not let your dog intimidate you and be so afraid of a bite that you can't discipline him. Professional help through your veterinarian, dog trainer and/or behaviorist can give you guidance.

HEALTH CARE

Veterinary medicine has become far more sophisticated than what was available to our ancestors. This can be attributed to the increase in household pets and consequently the demand for better care for them. Also human medicine has become far more complex. Today diagnostic testing in veterinary medicine parallels human diagnostics. Because of better technology we can expect our pets to live healthier lives thereby increasing their life spans.

THE FIRST CHECK UP

You will want to take your new puppy/dog in for its first check up within 48 to 72 hours after acquiring it. Many breeders strongly recommend this check up and so do the humane shelters. A puppy/dog can appear healthy but it may have a serious problem that is not apparent to the layman. Most pets have some type of a minor flaw that may never cause a real problem.

A healthy Chow will have the characteristic black tongue and mouth.

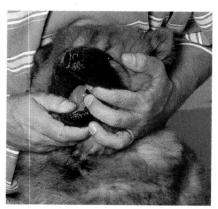

Unfortunately if he/she should have a serious problem, you will want to consider the consequences of keeping the pet and the attachments that will be formed, which may be broken prematurely. Keep in mind there are many healthy dogs looking for good homes.

This first check up is a good time to establish yourself with the veterinarian and learn the office policy regarding their hours and how they handle emergencies. Usually the breeder or another conscientious pet owner is a good

Good health care starts at the very beginning of your Chow puppies' lives. These little guys should be taken to the veterinarian within 48 to 72 hours of their big arrival.

reference for locating a capable veterinarian. You should be aware that not all veterinarians give the same quality of service. Please do not make your selection on the least expensive clinic, as they may be short changing your pet. There is the possibility that eventually it will cost you more due to improper diagnosis, treatment, etc. If you are selecting a new veterinarian, feel free to ask for a tour of the clinic. You should inquire about making an appointment for a tour since all clinics are working clinics, and therefore may not be available all day for sightseers. You may worry less if you see where your pet will be spending the day if he ever needs to be hospitalized.

THE PHYSICAL EXAM

Your veterinarian will check your pet's overall condition, which includes listening to the heart; checking the respiration; feeling the abdomen, muscles and joints; checking the mouth, which includes the gum color and signs of gum disease along with plaque buildup; checking the ears for signs of an infection or ear mites; examining the eyes; and, last but not least, checking the condition of the skin and coat.

He should ask you questions regarding your pet's eating and elimination habits and invite you to relay your questions. It is a good idea to prepare a list so as not to forget anything. He should discuss the proper diet and the quantity to be fed. If this should differ from your breeder's recommendation, then you should convey to him the breeder's choice and see if he approves. If he recommends changing the diet, then this should be done over a few days so as not to cause a gastrointestinal upset. It is customary to take in a fresh stool sample (just a small amount) for a test for intestinal parasites. It must be fresh, preferably within 12 hours, since the eggs hatch quickly and after hatching will not be observed under the microscope. If your pet isn't obliging then, usually the technician can take one in the clinic.

IMMUNIZATIONS

It is important that you take your puppy/dog's vaccination record with you on your first visit. In case of a puppy, presumably the breeder has seen to the vaccinations up to the time you acquired custody. Veterinarians differ in their vaccination protocol. It is not unusual for your puppy to have

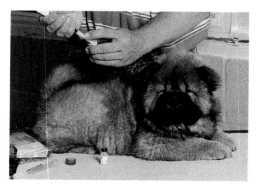

All puppies need to start at their vaccinations as soon as their veterinarian suggests.
Immunizations will protect your vulnerable puppy from many life-threatening diseases.

received vaccinations for distemper, hepatitis, leptospirosis, parvovirus and parainfluenza every two to three weeks from the age of five or six weeks. Usually this is a combined injection and is typically called the DHLPP. The DHLPP is given through at least 12 to 14 weeks of age, and it is customary to continue with another parvovirus vaccine at 16 to 18 weeks. You may wonder why so many immunizations are necessary. No one knows for sure when the puppy's maternal antibodies are gone, although it is customarily accepted that distemper antibodies are gone by 12 weeks. Usually parvovirus antibodies are gone by 16 to 18 weeks of age. However, it is possible for the maternal antibodies to be gone at a much earlier age or even a later age. Therefore immunizations are started at an early age. The vaccine will not give immunity as long as there are maternal antibodies.

The deer tick is the most common carrier of Lyme disease. Photo courtesy of Virbac Laboratories, Inc., Fort Worth, Texas.

The rabies vaccination is given at three or six months of age depending on your local laws. A vaccine for bordetella (kennel cough) is advisable and can be given anytime from the age of five weeks. The coronavirus is not commonly given unless there is a problem locally. The Lyme vaccine is necessary in endemic areas. Lyme disease has been reported in 47 states.

Distemper

This is virtually an incurable disease. If the dog recovers, he is subject to severe nervous disorders. The virus attacks every tissue in the body and resembles a bad cold with a fever. It can cause a runny nose and eyes and cause gastrointestinal disorders, including a poor appetite, vomiting and diarrhea. The virus is carried by raccoons, foxes, wolves, mink and other dogs. Unvaccinated youngsters and senior citizens are very susceptible. This is still a common disease.

Hepatitis

This is a virus that is most serious in very young dogs. It is spread by contact with an infected animal or its stool or urine.

The virus affects the liver and kidneys and is characterized by high fever, depression and lack of appetite. Recovered animals may be afflicted with chronic illnesses.

Leptospirosis

This is a bacterial disease transmitted by contact with the urine of an infected dog, rat or other wildlife. It produces severe symptoms of fever, depression, jaundice and internal bleeding and was fatal before the vaccine was developed. Recovered dogs can be carriers, and the disease can be transmitted from dogs to humans.

Parvovirus

This was first noted in the late 1970s and is still a fatal disease. However, with proper vaccinations, early diagnosis and prompt treatment, it is a manageable disease. It attacks the bone marrow

The great outdoors can hold many dangers for your Chow Chow. Make sure your pet has all his vaccinations before allowing him to play outside

and intestinal tract. The symptoms include depression, loss of appetite, vomiting, diarrhea and collapse. Immediate medical attention is of the essence.

Rabies
This is shed in the saliva and is carried by raccoons, skunks, foxes, other dogs and cats. It attacks nerve tissue, resulting in paralysis and death. Rabies can be transmitted to people and is virtually always fatal. This disease is reappearing in the suburbs.

Bordetella (Kennel Cough)
The symptoms are coughing, sneezing, hacking and retching accompanied by nasal discharge usually lasting from a few days to several weeks. There are several disease-producing organisms responsible for this disease. The present vaccines are helpful but do not protect for all the strains. It usually is not life threatening but in some instances it can progress to a serious bronchopneumonia. The disease is highly contagious. The vaccination should be given routinely for dogs that come in contact with other dogs, such as through boarding, training class or visits to the groomer.

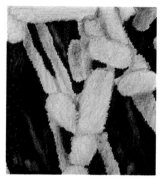

Bordetella attached to canine cilia. Otherwise known as kennel cough, this disease is highly contagious and should be vaccinated against routinely.

Coronavirus
This is usually self limiting and not life threatening. It was first noted in the late '70s about a year before parvovirus. The virus produces a yellow/brown stool and there may be depression, vomiting and diarrhea.

Lyme Disease
This was first diagnosed in the United States in 1976 in Lyme, CT in people who lived in close proximity to the deer tick. Symptoms may include acute lameness, fever, swelling of

joints and loss of appetite. Your veterinarian can advise you if you live in an endemic area.

After your puppy has completed his puppy vaccinations, you will continue to booster the DHLPP once a year. It is customary to booster the rabies one year after the first vaccine and then, depending on where you live, it should be boostered every year or every three years. This depends on your local laws. The Lyme and corona vaccines are boostered annually and it is recommended that the bordetella be boostered every six to eight months.

ANNUAL VISIT

I would like to impress the importance of the annual check up, which would include the booster vaccinations, check for intestinal parasites and test for heartworm. Today in our very busy world it is rush, rush and see "how much you can get for how little." Unbelievably, some non-veterinary businesses have entered into the vaccination business. More harm than good can come to your dog through improper vaccinations, possibly from inferior vaccines and/or the wrong schedule. More than likely you truly care about your companion dog and over the years you have devoted much time and expense to his well being. Perhaps you are unaware that a vaccination is not just a vaccination. There is more involved. Please, please follow through with regular physical examinations. It is so important for your veterinarian to know your dog and this is especially true during middle age through the geriatric years. More than likely your older dog will require more than one physical a year. The annual physical is good preventive medicine. Through early diagnosis and subsequent treatment your dog can maintain a longer and better quality of life.

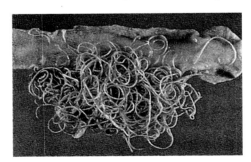

Roundworms are spaghetti-like worms that cause a potbellied appearance and dull coat, along with diarrhea and vomiting. Photo courtesy of Merck AgVet.

Hookworms

These are almost microscopic intestinal worms that can cause anemia and therefore serious problems, including death, in young puppies. Hookworms can be transmitted to humans through penetration of the skin. Puppies may be born with them.

Roundworms

These are spaghetti-like worms that can cause a potbellied appearance and dull coat along with more severe symptoms, such as

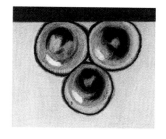

Roundworm eggs, as would be seen on a fecal evaluation. The eggs must develop for at least 12 days before they are infective.

vomiting, diarrhea and coughing. Puppies acquire these while in the mother's uterus and through lactation. Both hookworms and roundworms may be acquired through ingestion.

Whipworms

These have a three-month life cycle and are not acquired through the dam. They cause intermittent diarrhea usually with mucus. Whipworms are possibly the most difficult worm to eradicate. Their eggs are very resistant to most environmental factors and can last for years until the proper conditions enable them to mature. Whipworms are seldom seen in the stool.

Intestinal parasites are more prevalent in some areas than others. Climate, soil and contamination are big factors contributing to the incidence of intestinal parasites. Eggs are passed in the stool, lay on the ground and then become infective in a certain number of days. Each of the above worms has a different life cycle. Your best chance of becoming and remaining worm-free is to always pooper-scoop your yard. A fenced-in yard keeps stray dogs out, which is certainly helpful.

I would recommend having a fecal examination on your dog twice a year or more often if there is a problem. If your dog has a positive fecal sample, then he will be given the appropriate medication and you will be asked to bring back another stool sample in a certain period of time (depending on the type of worm) and then be rewormed. This process goes on until he has at least two negative samples. The different types of worms require different medications. You will be wasting your money and doing your dog an injustice by buying over-the-counter medication without first consulting your veterinarian.

OTHER INTERNAL PARASITES

Coccidiosis and Giardiasis

These protozoal infections usually affect puppies, especially in places where large numbers of puppies are brought together. Older dogs may harbor these infections but do not show signs unless they are stressed. Symptoms include diarrhea, weight loss and lack of appetite. These infections are not always apparent in the fecal examination.

Tapeworms

Seldom apparent on fecal floatation, they are diagnosed frequently as rice-like segments around the dog's anus and the base of the tail. Tapeworms are long, flat and ribbon like, sometimes several feet in length, and made up of many segments about five-eighths of an inch long. The two most common types of tapeworms found in the dog are:

(1) First the larval form of the flea tapeworm parasite must mature in an intermediate host, the flea, before it can become infective. Your dog acquires this by ingesting the flea through licking and chewing.

(2) Rabbits, rodents and certain large game animals serve as intermediate hosts for other species of tapeworms. If your dog should eat one of these infected hosts, then he can acquire tapeworms.

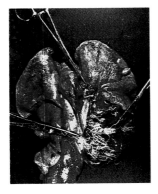

Dirofilaria - adult worms in the heart of a dog. It is possible for a dog to be infected with any number of worms from one to a hundred. Courtesy of Merck AgVet.

Puppies can be born infected with worms so all should be presumed potential carriers and treated with a worm control regimen.

HEARTWORM DISEASE

This is a worm that resides in the heart and adjacent blood vessels of the lung that produces microfilaria, which circulate in the bloodstream. It is possible for a dog to be infected with any number of worms from one to a hundred that can be 6 to 14 inches long. It is a life-threatening disease, expensive to treat and easily prevented. Depending on where you live, your veterinarian may recommend a preventive year-round and either an annual or semiannual blood test. The most common preventive is given once a month.

EXTERNAL PARASITES

Fleas

These pests are not only the dog's worst enemy but also enemy to the owner's pocketbook. Preventing is less expensive than treating, but regardless I think we'd prefer to spend our money elsewhere. I would guess that the majority of our dogs are allergic to the bite of a flea, and in many cases it only takes one flea bite. The protein in the flea's saliva is the culprit. Allergic dogs have a reaction, which usually results in a "hot spot." More than likely such a reaction will involve a trip to the veterinarian for treatment. Yes, prevention is less expensive. Fortunately today there are several good products available.

If there is a flea infestation, no one product is going to correct the problem. Not only will the dog require treatment so will the environment. In general flea collars are not very effective although there is now available an "egg" collar that will kill the eggs on the dog. Dips are the most economical but they are messy. There are some effective shampoos and treatments available through pet shops and veterinarians. An oral tablet arrived on the American market in 1995

All Chows should be checked carefully for any signs of fleas or ticks after they have been playing outside.

and was popular in Europe the previous year. It sterilizes the female flea but will not kill adult fleas. Therefore the tablet, which is given monthly, will decrease the flea population but is not a "cure-all." Those dogs that suffer from flea-bite allergy will still be subjected to the bite of the flea. Another popular parasiticide is permethrin, which is applied to the back of the dog in one or two places depending on the dog's weight. This product works as a repellent causing the flea to get "hot feet" and jump off. Do not confuse this product with some of the organophosphates that are also applied to the dog's back.

The cat flea is the most common flea of both dogs and cats. Courtesy of Fleabusters, Rx for Fleas, Inc., Fort Lauderdale, Florida.

Some products are not usable on young puppies. Treating fleas should be done under your veterinarian's guidance. Frequently it is necessary to combine products and the layman does not have the knowledge regarding possible toxicities. It is hard to believe but there are a few dogs that do have a natural resistance to fleas. Nevertheless it would be wise to treat all pets at the same time. Don't forget your cats. Cats just love to prowl the neighborhood and consequently return with unwanted guests.

Adult fleas live on the dog but their eggs drop off the dog into the environment. There they go through four larval stages before reaching adulthood, and thereby are able to jump back on the poor unsuspecting dog. The cycle resumes and takes between 21 to 28 days under ideal conditions. There are environmental products available that will kill both the adult fleas and the larvae.

Ticks

Ticks carry Rocky Mountain Spotted Fever, Lyme disease and can cause tick paralysis. They should be removed with tweezers, trying to pull out the head. The jaws carry disease. There is a tick preventive collar that does an excellent job. The ticks automatically back out on those dogs wearing collars.

Sarcoptic Mange

This is a mite that is difficult to find on skin scrapings. The pinnal reflex is a good indicator of this disease. Rub the ends of the pinna (ear) together and the dog will start scratching with his foot. Sarcoptes are highly contagious to other dogs and to humans although they do not live long on humans. They cause intense itching.

Demodectic Mange

This is a mite that is passed from the dam to her puppies. It affects youngsters age three to ten months. Diagnosis is confirmed by skin scraping. Small areas of alopecia around the eyes, lips and/or forelegs become visible. There is little itching unless there is a secondary bacterial infection. Some breeds are afflicted more than others.

All Chows should be screened for genetic defects before being bred in order to ensure healthy offspring and preserve the quality of the breed.

Cheyletiella

This causes intense itching and is diagnosed by skin scraping. It lives in the outer layers of the skin of dogs, cats, rabbits and humans. Yellow-gray scales may be found on the back and the rump, top of the head and the nose.

TO BREED OR NOT TO BREED

More than likely your breeder has requested that you have your puppy neutered or spayed. Your breeder's request is based on what is healthiest for your dog and what is most beneficial for your breed. Experienced and conscientious breeders devote many years into developing a bloodline. In order to do this, he makes every effort to plan each breeding in regard to conformation, temperament and health. This type of breeder does his best to perform

Low-lying tree branches and high grasses are perfect places for ticks to hide. If you find any ticks on your Chow, remove them promptly and carefully.

the necessary testing (i.e., OFA, CERF, testing for inherited blood disorders, thyroid, etc.). Testing is expensive and sometimes very disheartening when a favorite dog doesn't pass his health tests. The health history pertains not only to the breeding stock but to the immediate ancestors. Reputable breeders do not want their offspring to be bred indiscriminately. Therefore you may be asked to neuter or spay your puppy. Of course there is always the exception, and your breeder may agree to let you breed your dog under his direct supervision. This is an important concept. More and more effort is being made to breed healthier dogs.

Spay/Neuter

There are numerous benefits of performing this surgery at six months of age. Unspayed females are subject to mammary and ovarian cancer. In order to prevent mammary cancer she must be spayed prior to her first heat cycle. Later in life, an unspayed female may develop a pyometra (an infected uterus), which is definitely life threatening.

Spaying is performed under a general anesthetic and is easy on the young dog. As you might expect it is a little harder on the older dog, but that is no reason to deny her the surgery. The surgery removes the ovaries and uterus. It is important to remove all the ovarian tissue. If some is left behind, she could remain attractive to males. In order to view the ovaries, a reasonably long incision is necessary. An ovariohysterectomy is considered major surgery.

Neutering the male at a young age will inhibit some characteristic male behavior that owners frown upon. I have found my boys will not hike their legs and mark territory if they are neutered at six months of age. Also neutering at a young age has hormonal benefits, lessening the chance of hormonal aggressiveness.

Surgery involves removing the testicles but leaving the scrotum. If there should be a retained testicle, then he definitely needs to be neutered before the age of two or three years. Retained testicles can develop into cancer. Unneutered males are at risk for testicular cancer, perineal fistulas, perianal tumors and fistulas and prostatic disease.

Intact males and females are prone to housebreaking accidents. Females urinate frequently before, during and after heat cycles, and males tend to mark territory if there is a female in heat. Males may show the same behavior if there is a visiting dog or guests.

Surgery involves a sterile operating procedure equivalent to human surgery. The incision site is shaved, surgically scrubbed and draped. The veterinarian wears a sterile surgical gown, cap, mask and gloves. Anesthesia should be monitored by a registered technician. It is customary for the veterinarian to recommend a pre-anesthetic blood screening, looking for metabolic problems and a ECG rhythm strip to check for normal heart function. Today anesthetics are equal to human anesthetics, which enables your dog to walk out of the clinic the same day as surgery.

Some folks worry about their dog gaining weight after being neutered or spayed. This is usually not the case. It is true that some dogs may be less active so they could develop a problem, but my own dogs are just as active as they were before surgery. I have a hard time keeping weight on them. However, if your dog should begin to gain, then you need to decrease his food and see to it that he gets a little more exercise.

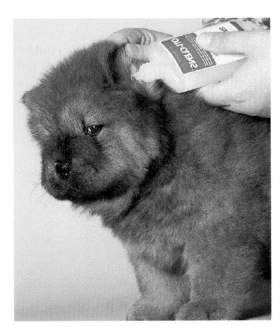

Keeping your Chow's ears clean and free of waxy build-up is just one of the many steps in practicing good preventive health care.

DENTAL CARE for Your Dog's Life

So you've got a new puppy! You also have a new set of puppy teeth in your household. Anyone who has ever raised a puppy is abundantly aware of these new teeth. Your puppy will chew anything it can reach, chase your shoelaces, and play "tear the rag" with any piece of clothing it can find. When puppies are newly born, they have no teeth. At about four weeks of age, puppies of most breeds begin to develop their deciduous or baby teeth. They begin eating semi-solid food, fighting and biting with their litter mates, and learning discipline from their mother. As their new teeth come in, they inflict more pain on their mother's breasts, so her feeding sessions become less frequent and shorter. By six or eight weeks, the mother will start growling to warn her pups when they are fighting too roughly or hurting her as they nurse too much with their new teeth.

Puppies need to chew. It is a necessary part of their physical and mental development. They develop muscles and necessary life skills as they drag objects around, fight over possession, and vocalize alerts and warnings. Puppies chew on things to explore their world. They are using their sense of taste to determine what is food and what is not. How else can they tell an electrical cord from a lizard? At about four months of age, most puppies begin shedding their baby teeth. Often these teeth need some help to come out and make way for the

Puppies need to chew in order to develop physically and mentally. Make sure your Chowlet has a safe Gumabone® to play with at all times.

permanent teeth. The incisors (front teeth) will be replaced first. Then, the adult canine or fang teeth erupt. When the baby tooth is not shed before the permanent tooth comes in, veterinarians call it a retained deciduous tooth. This condition will often cause gum infections by trapping hair and debris between the permanent tooth and the retained baby tooth. Nylafloss® is an excellent device for puppies to use. They can toss it, drag it, and chew on the many

Brushing your Chow's teeth is a necessary part of your pet's dental maintenance.

Your Chow will begin to lose his puppy teeth at about four months of age. Giving your puppy adequate chew toys will aid in their removal. Fingers, of course, don't count!

Let your Chow do his part in keeping his teeth clean by allowing him to chew on a Carrot Bone® by Nylabone®. It is a durable chew containing no plastics or artificial ingredients. surfaces it presents. The baby teeth can catch in the nylon material, aiding in their removal. Puppies that have adequate chew toys will have less destructive behavior, develop more physically, and have less chance of retained deciduous teeth.

During the first year, your dog should be seen by your veterinarian at regular intervals. Your veterinarian will let you know when to bring in your puppy for vaccinations and parasite examinations. At each visit, your veterinarian should inspect the lips, teeth, and mouth as part of a complete physical examination. You should take some part in the maintenance of your dog's oral health. You should examine your dog's mouth weekly throughout his first year to make sure there are no sores, foreign objects, tooth problems, etc. If your dog drools excessively, shakes its head, or has bad breath, consult your veterinarian. By the time your dog is six months old, the permanent teeth are all in and plaque can start to accumulate on the tooth surfaces. This is when your dog needs to develop good dental-care habits to prevent calculus build-up on its teeth. Brushing is best. That is a fact that cannot be denied. However, some dogs do not like their teeth brushed regularly, or you may not be able to accomplish the task. In that case, you should consider a product that will help prevent plaque and calculus build-up.

The Plaque Attackers® and Galileo Bone® are other excellent choices for the first three years of a dog's life. Their shapes make them interesting for the dog. As the dog chews on them, the solid polyurethane massages the gums which improves the blood circulation to the periodontal tissues. Projections on the chew devices increase the surface and are in contact with the tooth for more efficient cleaning. The unique shape and consistency prevent your dog from exerting excessive force on his own teeth or from breaking off pieces of the bone. If your dog is an aggressive chewer or weighs more than 55 pounds (25 kg), you should consider giving him a Nylabone®, the most durable chew product on the market.

Your veterinarian should examine your Chow's mouth, gums and teeth as part of his physical examination.

The Gumabones ®, made by the Nylabone Company, is constructed of strong polyurethane, which is softer than nylon. Less powerful chewers prefer the Gumabones® to the Nylabones®. A super option for your dog is the Hercules Bone®, a uniquely shaped bone named after the great Olympian for its exception strength. Like all Nylabone products, they are specially scented to make them attractive to your dog. Ask your veterinarian about these bones and he will validate the good doctor's prescription: Nylabones® not only give your dog a good chewing workout but also help to save your dog's teeth (and even his life, as it protects him from possible fatal periodontal diseases).

By the time dogs are four years old, 75% of them have periodontal disease. It is the most common infection in dogs. Yearly examinations by your veterinarian are essential to maintaining your dog's good health. If your veterinarian detects periodontal disease, he or she may recommend a prophylactic cleaning. To do a thorough cleaning, it will be necessary to put your dog under anesthesia. With modern gas anesthetics and monitoring equipment, the procedure is pretty safe. Your veterinarian will scale the teeth with an ultrasound scaler or hand instrument. This removes the calculus from the teeth. If there are calculus deposits below the gum line, the veterinarian will plane the roots to make them smooth. After all of the calculus has been removed, the teeth are polished with pumice in a polishing cup. If any medical or surgical treatment is needed, it is done at this time. The final step would be fluoride treatment and your follow-up treatment at home. If the periodontal disease is advanced, the veterinarian may prescribe a medicated mouth rinse or antibiotics for use at home. Make sure your dog has safe, clean and attractive chew toys and treats. Chooz® treats are another way of using a consumable treat to help keep your dog's teeth clean.

Rawhide is the most popular of all materials for a dog to chew. This has never been good news to dog owners, because rawhide is inherently very dangerous for dogs. Thousands of dogs have died from rawhide, having swallowed the hide after it has become soft and mushy, only to cause stomach and intestinal blockage. A new rawhide product on the market has finally solved the problem of rawhide: molded Roar-Hide® from Nylabone. These are composed of processed, cut up, and melted American rawhide injected into your dog's favorite shape: a dog bone. These dog-safe devices smell and taste

A dental cleaning by a professional should be done at least annually. It is an important part of the fight against periodontal disease.

Roar-Hide™ by Nylabone® is the safe alternative to rawhide. It is melted and molded so it will not break up into harmful pieces, and it is 86.2% protein.

like rawhide but don't break up. The ridges on the bones help to fight tartar build-up on the teeth and they last ten times longer than the usual rawhide chews.

As your dog ages, professional examination and cleaning should become more frequent. The mouth should be inspected at least once a year. Your veterinarian may recommend visits every six months. In the geriatric patient, organs such as the heart, liver, and kidneys do not function as well as when they were young. Your veterinarian will probably want to test these organs' functions prior to using general anesthesia for dental cleaning. If your dog is a good chewer and you work closely with your veterinarian, your dog can keep all of its teeth all of its life. However, as your dog ages, his sense of smell, sight, and taste will diminish. He may not have the desire to chase, trap or chew his toys. He will also not have the energy to chew for long periods, as arthritis and periodontal disease make chewing painful. This will leave you with more responsibility for keeping his teeth clean and healthy. The dog that would not let you brush his teeth at one year of age, may let you brush his teeth now that he is ten years old.

If you train your dog with good chewing habits as a puppy, he will have healthier teeth throughout his life.

IDENTIFICATION and Finding the Lost Dog

There are several ways of identifying your dog. The old standby is a collar with dog license, rabies, and ID tags. Unfortunately collars have a way of being separated from the dog and tags fall off. I am not suggesting you shouldn't use a collar and tags. If they stay intact and on the dog, they are the quickest way of identification.

For several years owners have been tattooing their dogs. Some tattoos use a number with a registry. Here lies the problem because there are several registries to check. If you wish to tattoo, use your social security number. The humane shelters have the means to trace it. It is usually done on the inside of the rear thigh. The area is first shaved

The newest method of identification is microchipping. The microchip is a computer chip that is no bigger than a grain of rice.

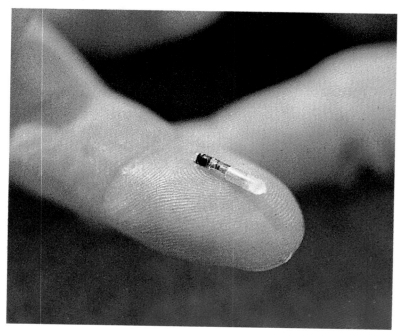

Always keep a leash and collar on your dog when you venture outdoors. Identification tags will help you reunite with your pet should you become separated.

and numbed. There is no pain, although a few dogs do not like the buzzing sound. Occasionally tattooing is not legible and needs to be redone.

The newest method of identification is microchipping. The microchip is a computer chip that is no larger than a grain of rice. The veterinarian implants it by injection between the shoulder blades. The dog feels no discomfort. If your dog is lost and picked up by the humane society, they can trace you by scanning the microchip, which has its own code. Microchip scanners are friendly to other brands of microchips and their registries. The microchip comes with a dog tag saying the dog is microchipped. It is the safest way of identifying your dog.

FINDING THE LOST DOG

I am sure you will agree with me that there would be little worse than losing your dog. Responsible pet owners rarely lose their dogs. They do not let their dogs run free because they don't want harm to come to them. Not only that but in most, if not all, states there is a leash law.

Beware of fenced-in yards. They can be a hazard. Dogs find ways to escape either over or under the fence. Another fast exit is through the gate that perhaps the neighbor's child left unlocked.

It is useful to have a good, clear photograph of your dog on hand to help identify him if he ever becomes lost.

Below is a list that hopefully will be of help to you if you need it. Remember don't give up, keep looking. Your dog is worth your efforts.

1. Contact your neighbors and put flyers with a photo on it in their mailboxes. Information you should include would be the dog's name, breed, sex, color, age, source of identification, when your dog was last seen and where, and your name and phone numbers. It may be helpful to say the dog needs medical care. Offer a *reward*.
2. Check all local shelters daily. It is also possible for your dog to be picked up away from home and end up in an out-of-the-way shelter. Check these too. Go in person. It is not good enough to call. Most shelters are limited on the time they can hold dogs then they are put up for adoption or euthanized. There is the possibility that your dog will not make it to the shelter for several days. Your dog could have been wandering or someone may have tried to keep him.
3. Notify all local veterinarians. Call and send flyers.
4. Call your breeder. Frequently breeders are contacted when one of their breed is found.
5. Contact the rescue group for your breed.
6. Contact local schools—children may have seen your dog.
7. Post flyers at the schools, groceries, gas stations, convenience stores, veterinary clinics, groomers and any other place that will allow them.
8. Advertise in the newspaper.
9. Advertise on the radio.

TRAVELING with Your Dog

The earlier you start traveling with your new puppy or dog, the better. He needs to become accustomed to traveling. However, some dogs are nervous riders and become carsick easily. It is helpful if he starts with an empty stomach. Do not despair, as it will go better if you continue taking him with you on short fun rides. How would you feel if every time you rode in the car you stopped at the doctor's for an injection? You would soon dread that nasty car. Older dogs that tend to get carsick may have more of a problem adjusting to traveling. Those dogs that are having a serious problem may benefit from some medication prescribed by the veterinarian.

Do give your dog a chance to relieve himself before getting into the car. It is a good idea to be prepared for

Some dogs may have a harder time adjusting to traveling, so the earlier you bring your Chow for car rides, the better. This Chow has gotten really accustomed to his owner's car!

a clean up with a leash, paper towels, bag and terry cloth towel.

The safest way for your dog to travel in a car is in a crate. If your accustom your dog to his crate at home, he will feel much more comfortable.

The safest place for your dog is in a fiberglass crate, although close confinement can promote carsickness in some dogs. If your dog is nervous you can try letting him ride on the seat next to you or in someone's lap.

An alternative to the crate would be to use a car harness made for dogs and/or a safety strap attached to the harness or collar. Whatever you do, do not let your dog ride in the back of a pickup truck unless he is securely tied on a very short lead. I've seen trucks stop quickly and, even though the dog was tied, it fell out and was dragged.

I do occasionally let my dogs ride loose with me because I really enjoy their companionship, but in all honesty they are safer in their crates. I have a friend whose van rolled in

an accident but his dogs, in their fiberglass crates, were not injured nor did they escape. Another advantage of the crate is that it is a safe place to leave him if you need to run into the store. Otherwise you wouldn't be able to leave the windows down. Keep in mind that while many dogs are overly protective in their crates, this may not be enough to deter dognappers. In some states it is against the law to leave a dog in the car unattended.

Never leave a dog loose in the car wearing a collar and leash. I have known more than one dog that has killed himself by hanging. Do not let him put his head out an open window. Foreign debris can be blown into his eyes. When leaving your dog unattended in a car, consider the temperature. It can take less than five minutes to reach temperatures over 100 degrees Fahrenheit.

Boarding your dog in a kennel is one option you might consider if you are going away.

TRIPS

Perhaps you are taking a trip. Give consideration to what is best for your dog—traveling with you or boarding. When traveling by car, van or motor home, you need to think ahead about locking your vehicle. In all probability you have many valuables in the car and do not wish to leave it unlocked. Perhaps most valuable and not replaceable is your dog. Give thought to securing your vehicle and providing adequate ventilation for him. Another consideration for you when traveling with your dog is medical problems that may arise and little inconveniences, such as exposure to external parasites. Some areas of the country are quite flea infested. You

Many airlines and hotels have restrictions regarding traveling with pets. Make sure you investigate these before bringing your Chow along.

may want to carry flea spray with you. This is even a good idea when staying in motels. Quite possibly you are not the only occupant of the room.

Unbelievably many motels and even hotels do allow canine guests,

155

even some very first-class ones. Gaines Pet Foods Corporation publishes *Touring With Towser*, a directory of domestic hotels and motels that accommodate guests with dogs. Their address is Gaines TWT, PO Box 5700, Kankakee, IL, 60902. I would recommend you call ahead to any motel that you may be considering and see if they accept pets. Sometimes it is necessary to pay a deposit against room damage. Of course you are more likely to gain accommodations for a small dog than a large dog. Also the management feels reassured when you mention that your dog will be crated. Since my dogs tend to bark when I leave the room, I leave the TV on nearly full blast to deaden the noises outside that tend to encourage my dogs to bark. If you do travel with your dog, take along plenty of baggies so that you can clean up after him. When we all do our share in cleaning up, we make it possible for motels to continue accepting our pets. As a matter of fact, you should practice cleaning up everywhere you take your dog.

Depending on where your are traveling, you may need an up-to-date health certificate issued by your veterinarian. It is good policy to take along your dog's medical information, which would include the name, address and phone number of your veterinarian, vaccination record, rabies certificate, and any medication he is taking.

AIR TRAVEL

When traveling by air, you need to contact the airlines to check their policy. Usually you have to make arrangements up to a couple of weeks in advance for traveling with your dog. The airlines require your dog to travel in an airline approved fiberglass crate. Usually

If you take your Chow with you on vacation, bring along something familiar to make him feel comfortable.

A reputable boarding kennel will require that dogs receive the vaccination for kennel cough no less than two weeks before their scheduled stay.

these can be purchased through the airlines but they are also readily available in most pet-supply stores. If your dog is not accustomed to a crate, then it is a good idea to get him acclimated to it before your trip. The day of the actual trip you should withhold water about one hour ahead of departure and no food for about 12 hours. The airlines generally have temperature restrictions, which do not allow pets to travel if it is either too cold or too hot. Frequently these restrictions are based on the temperatures at the departure and arrival airports. It's best to inquire about a health certificate. These usually need to be issued within ten days of departure. You should arrange for non-stop, direct flights and if a commuter plane should be involved, check to see if it will carry dogs. Some don't. The Humane Society of the United States has put together a tip sheet for airline traveling. You can receive a copy by sending a self-addressed stamped envelope to:

The Humane Society of the United States
Tip Sheet
2100 L Street NW
Washington, DC 20037.

Regulations differ for traveling outside of the country and are sometimes changed without notice. Well in advance you need to write or call the appropriate consulate or agricultural department for instructions. Some countries have lengthy quarantines (six months), and countries differ in their rabies vaccination requirements. For instance, it may have to be given at least 30 days ahead of your departure.

Do make sure your dog is wearing proper identification. You never know when you might be in an accident and separated from your dog. Or your dog could be frightened and somehow manage to escape and run away. When I travel, my dogs wear collars with engraved nameplates with my name, phone number and city.

Another suggestion would be to carry in-case-of-emergency instructions. These would include the address and phone number of a relative or friend, your veterinarian's name, address and phone number, and your dog's medical information.

BOARDING KENNELS

Perhaps you have decided that you need to board your dog. Your veterinarian can recommend a good boarding facility or possibly a pet sitter that will come to your house. It is customary for the boarding kennel to ask for proof of vaccination for the DHLPP, rabies and bordetella vaccine. The bordetella should have been given within six months of boarding. This is for your protection. If they do not ask for this proof I would not board at their kennel. Ask about flea control. Those dogs that suffer flea-bite allergy can get in trouble at a boarding kennel. Unfortunately boarding kennels are limited on how much they are able to do.

For more information on pet sitting, contact NAPPS: National Association of Professional Pet Sitters
1200 G Street, NW
Suite 760
Washington, DC 20005.

Our clinic has technicians that pet sit and technicians that board clinic patients in their homes. This may be an alternative for you. Ask your veterinarian if they have an employee that can help you. There is a definite advantage of having a technician care for your dog, especially if your dog is on medication or is a senior citizen.

You can write for a copy of *Traveling With Your Pet* from ASPCA, Education Department, 441 E. 92nd Street, New York, NY 10128.

SUGGESTED READING

H-965
Book of the Chow Chow
600 pages, over 500 photos.

TS-149
The World of The Chow Chow
528 pages, over 700 photos.

PS-812
The Chow Chow
256 pages, over 500 photos.

TS-214
Owner's Guide to Dog Health
432 pages, over 300 photos.

INDEX